Adam's Rib

Adam's Rib

RUTH HERSCHBERGER

HAR/ROW BOOKS
Harper & Row, Publishers
New York, Evanston, and London

ADAM'S RIB

This book was originally published by Pellegrini & Cudahy in New York in 1948. It was first published in England by Allen & Unwin Ltd. in 1954. It is here reprinted by arrangement.

First HAR/ROW edition published 1970
by Harper & Row, Publishers, Inc., 49 East 33rd Street,
New York, N.Y. 10016.

contents

Contents

To G. E. H.

author's note

This book appeared in 1948 but was written from about 1941 to 1946. Now women's liberation is a reality and it is good to see it brought out again, in this year of our lord 1970. The notes of a native feminist, it's still true, at least it seems so to me.

R. H.

preface

Ever since the beautiful story in Eden, recounting the fall of Adam through the fault of Eve, authors have not hesitated to employ woman in the role of villain or malefactor where the success of their drama depended on it. In the dramatization that follows, a similar source of misery was needed, to beset the protagonist Eve. This role has unhappily fallen to the lot of man.

Since all dramatization leads to exaggeration, the term "men" should not be taken in its more comprehensive sense. Rather was it feared that a cumbersome use of qualifiers—such as some, many, several, eight, eighteen, eighteen hundred, a few men —would impair the flow of the narrative. These have been waived, therefore, and the reader left free to assume them according to her (or his) own observations—which in this realm create their own absolute anyway.

If not otherwise specified, the term "men" is best taken in the standard sense of the English plural, to wit, "more than one."

CHAPTER ONE

how to tell a woman from a man

This hour I tell things in confidence;
I might not tell everybody, but I will tell you.

WHITMAN

To study recent books on the differences between
the sexes is to lose oneself in such a mass of trivia
that the primary sex difference, what Flaubert called
ce brave organe génital, is apt to be overlooked during the detailed discussion of fingerprints, heights,
weights, ball-throwing pattern, and the comparative
rate of ossification of the *epiphysis of calcaneus,* or
heel bone, in boys and girls.

As important as the differences in sex organs—the
books imply—is that the mature male should possess broad squared shoulders, heavy brows, straight
arms, narrow hips, cylindrical thighs, blunt toes and
bulging calves. The mature female is characterized
by soft sloping shoulders, a short neck, bent arms,
wide hips, conical thighs, small feet and knock-
knees. To insure understanding, illustrations are
provided, the man looking as though he had been
plagiarized out of a Bernarr Macfadden testimonial
and the woman out of the Rubens Gallery at Sara-
sota.

These, then, are the True Male and the True Female, the average, the typical, the normal, and to judge by a look around us, possibly the extinct.

For these representatives of the basic differences between the sexes appear to have been put together by calipers and glue rather than by the shakier hands of Mother Nature. While statistical facts helped evolve these sexual stereotypes, the Facts were crossbred with selected Ideals, probably for the noblest eugenic purposes. What we find sketched therefore is not so much the average man and woman as an ideal man and an ideal woman.

Where did the notion originate that a statistical majority promptly erects an esthetic standard of desirability? Did scientists know when they stated that men normally have broad squared shoulders and bulging calves that they would be laying down a criterion of beauty and purpose?

The word *normally*, in the biological sciences, means that a certain phenomenon is statistically common.[1] This is all it should mean. If what happens to be most common, by benefit of a 51 percent majority, is called the normal, and by implication the solely desirable, then what is statistically uncommon will be called abnormal, and by implication suspicious, imperfect, even dangerous.

If one standard of measurement after another, hundreds of them, of Mean Averages and majority ideals, were taken up, and in each case the minority and the deviant massacred as being abnormal and thus interfering with a stable and homogeneous society, there would not be one of us left standing in a fortnight.

Mankind, the erector of tyrannous Norms, is likewise fertile in the discovery of alternatives and in the tolerance of differences. Perhaps this is a whisper from the soul of man himself, for he too was once an alternative of suspicious origin. In a natural world dominated by the reptile and the dinosaur, this two-legged, apposite-thumbed monster sprang up—behold! Aristotle's rational man, who became the whole earth about whom the sun and moon were thought to lovingly revolve.

Yet in his earliest emergence, a rib from the missing link, man was an aberrant and chance mutation, statistically uncommon and therefore abnormal. Perhaps we should be more tolerant, as those ancestral dinosaurs were who did not expunge this vision of the future simply because he was unlike what had gone before.

CHAPTER TWO

josie takes the stand

*Public practice of any art, he observed, and staring
in men's faces, is very indelicate in a female.*

DR. JOHNSON *via* BOSWELL

Once upon a time there were two chimpanzees
called Josie and Jack. They lived in a cage in a chimpanzee colony in Orange Park, Florida. All day long
friendly scientists observed and made records of
them. This was extremely flattering to the chimpanzees, and when one of them solved a particularly
hard puzzle, he received a piece of banana as a reward. Life seemed ideal.

But suddenly a cloud passed over the happy colony. On March 15, 1939, as Josie stood resolutely
beside the food chute, she little realized that she
had become representative of all womanhood, a
model upon which personnel directors and police
captains could in the future base their decisions and
argue their case.

Nor did her cage-mate, Jack, as he elbowed her
gently aside, realize that he was from that moment
the incarnation of the dominant male, an inspira-
tion to all humans who sought "friendly masculine ascendancy" over their womenfolk.

For thirty-two successive days ten bits of banana,
at spaced intervals, slid down the food chute toward
the waiting chimpanzees. Who would get the tidbit

first? Who would demand it? Which animal, male or
female, would prove naturally dominant over the
other?

March 15: the first tidbit came down the chute
into the cage. Jack promptly claimed the food. Josie
did not protest; there was no physical conflict. Jack
ate all the food the first day, all of it the second, all
of it the third, and all but one bit the fourth.

Meanwhile, life and time were not at a standstill
for Josie. In the typical if egregious manner of the
female frame, her menstrual period had given way
to the post-menstrual, and this in turn withdrew in
favor of the period known as *tumescence* or genital
swelling. On March 21, as the swelling continued,
Josie abruptly appropriated all ten pieces of food,
much to Jack's displeasure. By March 23, Josie had
assumed command.

Josie retained the food chute in each daily experiment until April 3, when her period of tumescence
(and heat) was over and the genital swelling began
to subside. Thereafter the food chute was Jack's
(with one exception) until the termination of the
experiment.

By comparing the results of this experiment with
those from experiments with other mates, it was
found that during tumescence the female almost invariably took over the food chute and claimed all
the tidbits without interference from the male.
Science had made an interesting discovery; all that
remained was the routine work of communicating
the results to the public.

It can now be illustrated that semantical analysis
is not mere quibbling over the definitions of words;

it can uncover buried facts and alter the interpretation of evidence.

In a popular version of this experiment, *Chimpanzees, A Laboratory Colony*,[1] by Robert M. Yerkes, the one fact that emerged quite clearly was that Jack had made off with most of the honors. This was true enough, but issue can be taken with parts of the account, and particularly with the use of the word "natural," a variant of "normal." It is an ordinary little word, and yet it stands for so much in the mind of the public.

When human beings want to know what they're "really" like they turn to the lower animals, who are thought to exhibit impulses closer to nature, untainted by civilization and altogether more valid. Whatever turns out to be natural for the chimpanzee becomes practically conclusive for us.

From Josie and Jack's thirty-two days at the food chute, Professor Yerkes concluded not only that males were "naturally dominant" over females, but that the biological basis of prostitution stood revealed in certain aspects of Josie's behavior.

The matter was so disturbing that we took it directly to Josie. Josie was busy at the moment, grooming her friend Wendy, but on hearing of the manner in which the Thirty-Two Days had been presented to the reading public, Josie requested an opportunity to present her version of the affair.

The Interview

"People have been very kind to me at Orange Park," Josie began, "and I don't like to look a gift horse in the mouth. However, I would like to register a protest against the attempt to discredit my food chute score in the Thirty-Two Day test. Apparently all that humans want to hear is that Jack was dominant. *Why don't they ask what the score was?* You wouldn't slight the Brooklyn Dodgers that way, would you?

"Well, I'll tell you what the score was. I was top man at the food chute for fourteen days out of the thirty-two. Jack was top man for eighteen. This means I won 44 percent of the time, and Jack won 56 percent. He's champion, I'll grant you that; but still it's almost fifty-fifty. If Jack hadn't been dragged in as the *biggest* male in the whole colony . . . well, it sounds like sour grapes.

" 'When the female is not sexually receptive,' writes Professor Yerkes, 'the naturally more dominant member of the pair almost regularly obtains the food; whereas during the female's phase of maximal genital swelling, when she is sexually receptive, she claims or may claim the food and take it regularly even though she be the *naturally subordinate member* of the pair. . . .'

"What is this? Are there eight aces in this deck? The italics are not only mine, I'm proud of them. Those words," cried Josie, "look like somebody decided I was subordinate way in advance. The referees are practically saying any gains I make while I'm 'sexually receptive' can't be registered because the phase of maximal genital swelling is out of bounds!"

Josie lowered her voice to a whisper. "There are sinister implications in this, for human females as well as for the women in our colony. If the period of sexual interest is, by implication, an extra-natural phase in women (for it makes us *act* dominant when we're really *naturally* subordinate), it looks like we girl chimps spend about 14 days out of every 32 in the toils of Satan.

"It all comes from there being so few women scientists. Some woman scientist ought to start passing it around that males must be unnatural because they don't have cyclical changes during the month. Then see the furor start. Maybe they'll see how much fun it is being deviants half your life. Look:

" 'Under certain circumstances,' writes Professor Yerkes, 'the sexual relation of the mates may supplant natural dominance.'

"But what is so *unnatural* about the sexual relation of the mates!" exclaimed Josie. "I work up a good score, and they want to disqualify me because I happened to be feeling good! Besides," she continued, "why call me sexually receptive anyway? That's one of those human words with an opinion written all over it. Call me sexually interested if you will, for I am. In typical pre-mating activity, who starts everything by leading off at a run? And who decides when the parlor game stops and the male establishes contact? I do. Receptive? I'm about as receptive as a lion waiting to be fed!

"You know, human society is looking to us chimpanzees to set a pattern for the relation between the sexes, and it's hardly fair to misrepresent our social adjustments. Let's look at the circumstances of the experiment, for I don't think aspects of it were as controlled as they should be in the empirical sciences.

"Lots of factors make one chimp dominant over another. Weight is a big factor and hunger is another. Just because there's no physical conflict doesn't mean that force isn't the deciding factor. Chimpanzees understand each other just as humans do. If one of us really wants that food, don't think fightability can't be communicated by other means than swatting.

"When I got the food chute, it was because I wanted it bad enough. Maybe the time of sexual 'receptivity' makes the female more aggressive: that's a funny word-mix! When Jack got the food chute it wasn't because I didn't want it, but because I saw that he was willing to scrap for it. Perhaps when I was sexually receptive I was hungrier. You've got to remember that all during this test we had our regular meals every day; we weren't starved. Lots of the dominance was temperament. Take Wendy, a friend of mine. She's little and yet when she was tested with Bokar she fought him right along. She *cared*.

"When Jack takes over the food chute, the report calls it his 'natural dominance.' When I do, it's 'privilege'—conferred by him. If you humans could get enough perspective on your language, you'd find it as much fun as a zoo. While I'm up there lording it over the food chute, the investigator writes down 'the male temporarily defers to her and allows her to act as if dominant over him.' Can't I get any satisfaction out of life that isn't *allowed* me by some male chimp? Damn it!"

There were moments during the interview when Josie's language had to be taken to task.

"Don't interrupt," Josie said sharply. "It's this prostitution angle that makes me the maddest.* All

* "In the picture of behavior which is characteristic of femininity in the chimpanzee, the biological basis of prostitution of sexual function stands revealed. The mature and sexually ex-

sorts of higher primates are glomming on to the results of that food chute test, and their interpretation gets farther and farther from the facts, nearer and nearer to the corruptions typical of human society. Jack and I can go through almost the same motions, but by the time it gets down on paper, it has one name when Jack does it, and another if it was me.

"For instance, when Jack was at the chute and I gestured in sexual invitation to him, and after his acquiescence obtained the chute, this was put down as 'favor-currying' on my part, as exchanging sexual accommodation for food, as downright prostitution.

"Please note that on March 21, as well as on other occasions, Jack came up to me repeatedly at the chute and similarly gestured in sexual invitation. Doesn't this suggest that he was trying to get me away from the chute by carnal lure? Or was Jack just being (as everyone wants to think) an impulsive male? The experimenter took it as the latter. But who knows that Jack wasn't about to exchange sexual accommodation for food?

"The profoundest assumption behind all this is yet to be told. It's so unfair a girl hates to think of it. No matter what names you humans give to things, we chimpanzees go right on enjoying life. It isn't so with humans, and that's why I feel so sorry for women. The names you uncaged primates give things affect your attitude toward them forever after. You lose your insight because you are always holding up a screen of language between you and

perienced female trades upon her ability to satisfy the sexual urge of the male."—*Chimpanzees*, page 86.

the real world. Semantics tries to knock some chinks in this blind, and I'm all for it.

"The reason people are so sure that I traded sexual accommodation for food, and that Jack wouldn't, is because nobody thinks women enjoy love, I mean sex.

"It's as bad as that. People can't understand why any female animal should 'submit' (that's another of *your* words) to sex unless there's some reason for it—the reason here being to get control of those ten pieces of food!

"Maybe human females don't enjoy sex, but we chimps resent any forced analogy with humans. Among chimpanzees sex is controlled by the female, and don't let anyone tell you different.[2] The chimpanzee female doesn't permit sex unless she feels like it and you can talk sexual 'receptivity' the rest of your life, that word makes no impression on us unless we're inclined.

"Out of twenty-four females in our colony, two have consistently refused to mate. Don't ask me why; myself, I think they're crazy. All their cyclical changes look perfectly normal, and they get plenty of male attention too. But they just don't want to. How is it these two females haven't been raped by the overpowering males in the community? They haven't."

By this time Josie had hold of the bars of her cage and was sputtering excitedly. She harped on the fact that Jack was seventeen pounds heavier than she was, while the average male chimpanzee is only ten pounds heavier than the female. She kicked, too, because the only pairs tested for dominance were those in which the female was appreciably smaller.

"You can tell my listeners, too, that we chimpanzees are as different from one another as any bunch of human beings are. I don't like to see the word going around that prostitution or male dominance is 'characteristic of the apes.' You can take three numbers like 2 and 9 and 4, and say the average is 5, but that 5 isn't me and it isn't Wendy and it isn't Jack. It's a statistician's dream. If I need two pints of food a day and Jack needs four, don't try to satisfy either of us with three.

"And don't start saying three is 'normal' either," she cried.

"*De gustibus non est disputandum*. Wendy and I are as different as chromosomes can be, and we want to keep it that way. The human word *natural* and all its chaotic offspring—*feminine receptivity, friendly masculine ascendancy*, and the rest—are an obstruction of justice and an interference with nature."

Josie rested her case.

Not many laboratory experiments have been made on the innate differences between the sexes, though there has never been a dearth of big-game hunters, willing at the drop of a hat to discourse on the home life of the Bengal tiger. How often a hunter comes upon a domestic scene of love or hate or happy old age can be surmised. Yet whether he bagged so much as a weasel, a traveler from Africa or India can tell you exactly what the nuptial life of the leopard is like, or why prostitution is spreading among the jaguars.

Most of the reporters are males. One can also assume a selective process in favor of the mighty male, inclined to a tiger skin and the back of an elephant. We should not take too solemnly the reports of persons who are probably as ingenuous as you or I, except that they once had a ride through the jungle or spent an evening around a campfire chewing the rag about free love.

is rape a myth?

*Subtle he needs must be, who could seduce
Angels, nor think superfluous others' aid.*
MILTON: *Paradise Lost*

Rape as criminal assault is widespread, and distressingly so. In pointing out the respects in which rape is a myth, we are not indifferent to the crime itself. Rather is the crime being actively and invisibly supported by a legend of considerable glamor: the legend of man's natural sexual aggression toward women.

Rape is in this sense a mirror-image of our ordinary sex folkways. Two basic beliefs in these folkways are the natural sexual aggressiveness of man, and man's natural physical superiority over women. Put these two beliefs together, set up a competition for masculine prowess such as we have today, and no one should be surprised by the incidence of rape.

The typical description of man as aggressive, or *propulsive*, starts out amiably enough. In Karl Menninger's view, men have proportionately more of the death instinct, or the tendency to destroy. The dynamic essence of the masculine spirit is to make an impress upon something or someone.[1] This can lead to creativity or to death. (It is fair to say that it can also lead to rape.) The character of the result rests in the hands of woman.

Is this a flattering role for Adam's rib or not? It means that women must view themselves as a bundle of instincts aimed at neutralizing man's hostility and his tendency to self-destruction. In this scheme the achievements of man are due in part to the little woman.

More important: so are his failures. Should anything go wrong, as in the production of a Hitler, a woman is said to be at the root of the trouble—in this case, Hitler's mother. For if woman has a peculiar ability to interfere with the course of man's self-destructiveness,[2] it is her duty to devote her life to the mollification of this potential holocaust.

The so-called death instinct in men would seem to cover a multitude of sins. It is possible that society invented it expressly for this purpose. Anyone endowed with such an overdose of natural aggressiveness can scarcely be blamed for anything he may do, except for being too passive. Woman, gifted with a life instinct and the power of adaptability, is clearly the one to put up with the propulsiveness of man.

How much of these instincts is innate and how much acquired? If men can rape women, can women rape men? Can rape force a woman to respond or to feel pleasure? How is rape distinguished from a marriage in which the sex act is forced upon an unwilling woman? How does rape fit in with puritanism?

In exploring the ramifications of this subject we may find we are, in many cases, dealing less with a crime than with an ideal. To study "rape" as a lan-

guage symbol with high emotional content will be
rather like traveling through an exotic country filled
with ventriloquists, trolls, and fair princes. It is certainly not enough to leaf through a man-made dic-
tionary and examine the legal strait-jacket that has
been given the term.

Nor need we be misled by the ease with which
the forced and unwilling woman of the rape myth
becomes transformed into the affectionate and
grateful maiden. The legend of male aggressiveness
must be traced through all its avatars, finally to be
comprehended as a faith which secretly enlists many
educated minds in one of the happiest of male
fraternities.

She Stocked Her Heart
with Icy Frigidaire

Archimedes said that given a lever and a fixed
point, he could move the earth. With the leverage
provided by two words, *act* and *relationship*, the dichotomy of male and female sexuality is established
in the following description of rape.

> "No woman can force a man into the sex
> act," writes Amram Scheinfeld, "for his partici-
> pation in it requires a physical preparation which
> can come only with some degree of desire and
> willingness. . . . This is not so with a woman,
> for she can be forced into a sexual relationship
> without the least desire or preparedness." [8]

Josie warned us that the perfomance of an action
was typically given one name if she performed it,
and another name if Jack performed it. In the as-

signment of *the sex act* to man and a *sexual relationship* to woman, the same thing has taken place here.

Act implies something done, the exercise of power, the accomplishment of a deed. Thus, the sex act for a man implies a goal or climax which finds ultimate achievement. A relationship, on the other hand, is a condition or a state of being. It does not necessitate a goal or climax. An act is more impersonal than a relationship; it has fewer psychological complications. In a sexual relationship, a woman responds to the experience as a whole, and does not consider completion or relief its *raison d'être*. To a woman a sexual relationship is a more spiritual rapport, and is its own reason for being. Long after the male sex act is completed, the woman's relationship to the man continues.

In this simple, unconscious antithesis of act and relationship, we begin to understand why it is that the raped woman should suffer a permanent stain on her honor. In some occult way, she has been *forced* into a state of psychological identification or relationship with the person who criminally assaulted her.

The word *relationship* carries an undeniable implication of kinship. That a woman "can be forced into a sexual relationship without the least desire or preparedness" suggests that she can be involved in a psychological-sexual state of kinship with any man who successfully overpowers her.

Woman may resist, she may struggle, she may stock her heart with icy frigidaire (according to a popular song), but she is still forced to enter into a sexual *relationship*, provided her assailant is equipped with natural physical superiority—or a blackjack.

We are told that men, on the other hand, cannot be forced into a sexual relationship. In fact men's pride is as hurt by the thought that women might view sex as an "act," as that they themselves might enter into anything quite so confining, demanding, and sentimental as a "relationship."

The implications of the male act vs. the female relationship are as subtle as they are conclusive. The male act regards itself as single and indivisible, relatively unaffected by time, person, or place. It is therefore preceded by the definite article *the*; while a sexual relationship is feminine, diffuse, and employs the indefinite article.

Because it is so impossible for the masculine population to think of women in any connection except as responding to them, men are convinced that the raped victim, in spite of herself, responds in some degree to her assailant. No wonder a woman's purity is supposedly destroyed by a sex act forced upon her. She must enter into a sexual relationship with her aggressor; an intimacy with him is established for all time.

Can Women Rape Men?

Rape is a form of violence involving the personal humiliation of the victim. The act of rape is not simply an expression of sexual instinct. Rape is not practiced among the lower animals, but only among industrialized primates. Sexual intercourse if actually forced on an unwilling woman is a sadistic perversion that could as well be called "intravaginal

masturbation." This is a phrase which Menninger
uses in connection with narcissism; it applies even
more clearly to rape.

Murder is a form of violence forced upon an
unwilling victim; but murder does not humiliate its
victim, unless sexual elements are added. Not so
with the raped woman. She is rendered passive,
shamed, and dejected. While her relatives may decide to avenge her, they avenge only themselves.
Her attitude toward the episode remains conventionally one of despair, not resentment. Her honor
has been taken from her by force, and no recourse is
possible.

While a woman might "rape" a man in a highly
mechanical fashion, though no less mechanical than
the male type of assault,* she could not humiliate
him thereby. Society does not permit the removal of
a man's honor by force, lacking his consent or participation. A man could be forced to submit to the
indignity of sexual exploitation, but no one could
persuade him that he had been forced into a permanent relationship with his aggressor. He would
emerge from the experience socially unscathed.

When we consider that a virtuous woman,
resisting to the full extent of her physical strength,
is nevertheless robbed of her honor by violence, we
understand at least one respect in which women are
peculiarly at the mercy of higher powers in society.
With the extolling of woman's purity, men have

* If we regard ordinary rape as a form of "intravaginal masturbation," woman's "rape" of man would be extravaginal
masturbation. While she could not effect intromission, she
could effect orgasm. Rape typically implies the forced arousal
of the victim's emotions. This is inaccurate in any biological
sense, as will be explained later.

purported to put woman on a pedestal. What they have done is to take the defense of her honor out of her own hands, discourage her muscular reflexes, and virtually encourage various members of their sex to wage war on the purity that woman holds dear.

When women are commended for sustaining constancy, tenderness, and sympathy during the sex act, it is because they are taking care to concentrate on a psychological relationship, and not to assist in the performance of an act. The thought of a woman regarding the sex act as a means of finding sexual completion disturbs the soul. "It makes sex so mechanical!" exclaim men, who have all this time stressed the "automatic" and "impersonal" nature of their own sex impulse.

Indeed, if the receptivity of women were put in doubt for a moment, women might begin to think their own honor, as well as man's, was defensible. The carnage that would almost immediately result in buses, streetcars, theatres, and other places of public congregation would probably reduce the incidence of rape to a whisper.

The Weary Conqueror

The fun of being a conqueror has been greatly over-rated. The GIs in Germany and Japan are finding it out, and maybe the American husband and the American parent-mother will find it out too. The belief that aggression *per se* will iron out personality conflicts between human beings is equivalent to the belief that a sufficiently forceful war will eliminate the economic and social conflicts that caused the war. Much of the appeal of the rape myth stems from this worship of force.

When human beings, after much travail and tears, discover that force has not been particularly effective in solving a dilemma, nothing seems to prevent their hope that the next dilemma will be cured by a firmer application of the same nostrum. And there is always the possibility that the weaker factor in the conflict can be shut up for the time being.

In a polite way this has been happening in the conflicts between men and women. As women began to discover their own instincts and inclinations, husbands found their wives less and less amiable. The demands that were made in sensory matters alone contradicted everything a husband had been accustomed to expect from a wife. Soon there appeared on the market a succession of books, written by men, which asked eloquently that women be allowed to regain their ancient femininity, their receptivity of spirit; that they no longer be bothered with the chatter of emancipation.

The rape motif has made an interesting provision in its legend for this new development in the marriage mores. As women become more independent and recalcitrant in marriage, the vision of a woman who will actually, honestly, helplessly, and amiably submit to a man—because of applied force—cannot help appealing to the goaded and henpecked husband of the day. Here are the steps by which the rape myth wins over his mind.

Just as in the situation of rape, the man finds on his hands, secure within the bonds of marriage, an unwilling woman. It is true he picked her himself, but he may have done so at a time when all nice women were unwilling women, if they wished to remain members in good standing under the Purity Code. Let us use a bolder word, and call his unwilling woman frigid. She is frigid, but she is also vociferous, and gives her husband no peace. He would gladly satisfy her in any way he could; maybe it is his fault that he does not. Maybe it is her fault too, or her mother's fault or society's fault.

The unwilling woman submits to her husband's will, consistently and reluctantly, for twenty or thirty years. Meanwhile society permits her to express her unwillingness and resentment via the female institution of nagging. She may even acquire the enviable reputation of someone who runs her husband.

Society coincidentally seeks to divert the husband's dissatisfaction into safe channels. He is not unaware that his wife is sexually unwilling. After five or ten years he may toss this realization into his subconscious, but from the security of its new home the realization continues to plague him. He finally tells himself that sexual aggression toward women is the natural state of things, and he is only carrying out nature's plan.

The rape rumor can offer him something further. It not only agrees entirely that sexual aggression is the natural state, but it rather suspects that the natural woman is unwilling. It promises even more. For the rape myth conjures up an image of an unwilling stranger who, *unlike the unwilling wife*, instantly recognizes her assailant's right of sexual aggression— and loves him for it.

When the man turns to the sensational image of rape, he learns of a sex act which, if effected with any unwilling woman, can force her to enter into a sexual relationship with him. She can be forced into a psychological intimacy with him, as his wife stubbornly is not. Thus in the dream world of gross aggression, the husband finds the same unwilling woman of his marriage situation. But in the rape victim the unwilling woman magically becomes willing, her sensory nerves respond gratefully, stubborn reflexes react obediently, and the beautiful stranger willy-nilly enters into a state of sexual intimacy with her aggressor.

Who was it that initiated the belief that any application of pressure to an erogenous zone produces an experience of pleasure? We suspect it was a man married to a frigid wife. The notion that a victim of sexual aggression is forced into an experience of sensory delight should be relegated to the land where candy grows on trees and there are lemonade fountains. If any pressure applied to an erogenous zone resulted in pleasure, there would be no frigidity among women. If any pressure forced upon an erogenous zone resulted in pleasure, there would be no impotence among men.

The actual result of forced stimulation can be anesthesia or intense pain. This is true of the male if the stimulation is resisted or unwelcome. Yet the assumption that women are totally receptive has given rise to the belief that a rape victim cannot avoid feeling pleasure.

Were sensory nerves really this naïve, or were men's sexual apparatus as reflexive, automatic, and uncomplicated as some writers maintain, the rape of men by sexually aggressive women would be indeed possible. How could a man resist a woman who proved physically his superior? While the thought strikes us as ludicrous, it has never seemed particularly ludicrous to men that a woman should succumb with lightning speed to any force applied to her sensory centers.

The Logic of Wish

A logical positivist might be disturbed to see that our definition of rape is beginning to allow of an unwilling-women-who-is-willing. This explains why no symbolic logician will ever get to be president. he cannot be reconciled to the fact that one of the time-honored functions of language is to push reality into more pleasing shapes.

However, we might inquire whether rape, once it admits a victim who melts with pleasure and gratitude, is still to be considered true rape, rape *in extenso*, so to say. Or have we moved on by imperceptible degrees to a consideration of rape *inter se*?

Rape *inter se* is closer to seduction. However, no true disciple of the rape myth will hear of calling the phenomenon seduction, although the unwilling woman has, in his inner eye, long since become willing. He is not subscribing to a soul-satisfying myth, which mixes willingness and unwillingness in comforting proportions, in order to be told by some upstart logician that his myth is contradicting itself. The contradiction is put there for a purpose.

For the true subscriber cannot relinquish the idea of the unwillingness of the woman because it is her unwillingness that makes his carnality so marvelously free and impersonal. If he permits the unwilling woman to be willing right from the start, it isn't long before he finds himself worrying about keeping her happy or wondering what she is thinking of. This looks too much like home. He insists that the overpowered stranger be strictly unwilling.

At the same time the man cannot bear to think that the woman is not *actually* enjoying herself. For the stern aggressor actually has a heart of gold, and would like to satisfy in the person of this unknown woman all the women he has failed to satisfy in the realm of the real. He wants an unwilling woman who later becomes willing—under his magic touch.

Lonely men, unrequited men, men who find love and sex difficult turn to the myth of rape in the belief that love, if it cannot be evoked, can at least be bullied into putting in an appearance. But force and aggression drive love away as often as they serve to capture it. The tough men of the movies win their loves less by a brandishing of fists than by a restraint so marked as to approach indifference.

An appropriate warning to those who contemplate a wide choice of subjects in this myth-image is that forcing the sex act on a resistant woman requires more physical strength than may at first be supposed. It is difficult to know how often the frantic resistance of an unwilling woman is merely an attempt to whet the vigor of a mutual experience. In general a woman must be predisposed, or dyspeptic enough to be overcome. Where a strong and beautiful subject is selected, it might be necessary to render her unconscious first, in which case it is difficult to presume that she is psychologically implicated in the act.

The Purity of Force

To regard the sex act as sexual aggression is a sop to the puritan conscience. This may be observed in a typical description of sexual intercourse. A man is said to be attracted to the opposite sex by a natural impulse which is beyond his will. He performs an act in which a given reaction follows automatically. The male cannot help himself, he is obeying the forces of nature, and has little psychological involvement in what he does. He acts not through choice.

The man submits to the force of nature; the woman submits to the man. Sex is an act of aggression with which she complies only because she is physically the weaker. Her emphasis is on the future bearing and rearing of children which, according to Menninger, is woman's greatest achievement and the climax of her erotic expression. Being psychologically involved in the future, she is relatively free of implication in the present. She is thinking only of the children.

> Then call them not the Authors of their ill,
> No more than wax shall be accounted evil,
> Wherein is stamped the semblance of the Devil.

So much for *The Rape of Lucrece*. It applies as well to the puritanical woman today who sincerely believes that it is only her own helplessness that forces her to enter into a sexual relationship with a dominant member of the opposite sex.

CHAPTER FOUR

a minor mystery

To our bodies turn we then, that so
Weak men on love revealed may look;
Love's mysteries in souls do grow,
But yet the body is his book.

JOHN DONNE

Why is woman persistently regarded as a mystery? It is not that she has labored to conceal the organic and psychological facts of her constitution, but that men have showed no interest in exploring them. Indeed, a premium was early put on woman's remaining a mystery. It simplifies everything—if no woman knows what she wants, and if it is impossible for a mere man to understand what women want, the nuisance of discussion can be set aside.

Women are mysteries, intuitive as children, changeful as chameleons, loved but not understood.

The female early recognized the advantages in this portrait of herself. She set out, with very little mystery, to exploit the economic system according to the role assigned her, that of the inexplicable extravagant child, with a dash of Eve. In the lovelorn columns women are advised not to dispel their air of mystery and charm.

Much has been written of women's souls and little about their bodies. As John Donne remarks above, *Love's mysteries in souls do grow.* But no one has especially wanted to read women in cold print. Even the women themselves have realized what the dropping of the veil would mean: a threat to their present status as dependents. Only as it becomes more difficult for women in factories and offices to regard themselves as bewildered children or to derive a living from it, will there develop an impetus toward understanding the ABCs of women's constitution.

Metaphors have long figured in popular books on sex, partly out of deference to woman's modesty but also with the intention of promoting her mystery. One finds in the annals of love the leading vision of woman as a harp upon which the husband plays a melody. He is counseled to deal gently and considerately with the rare instrument of feminine loveliness, and books supply him with many instrumental hints regarding harmonics, technique, interpretation, crescendo, and the like.

The safety and security of this metaphor is that a harp doesn't talk back. One may elicit sour tones now and again, but the rest is silence. Masculine intellects have eagerly instructed one another in how to play this harp, but they have seldom asked the harp for advice. The time has come to consider whether women are not something more than passive instruments whose melodies are mere reflections of male dexterity.

The Lost Chord

In the symphony of love, the lost chord is a small organ lying somewhat north of the vagina. This entire zone is called the vulva, and includes all external genitals, labia, entrance to vagina, and the organ alluded to, the clitoris. The clitoris, hidden by a hoodlike fold of the labia, is so tiny and insignificant in size that various thinkers have referred to it, darkly, as the missing penis. Freud thought the phrase "the missing penis" was a good description of the difference between men and women. However, this is no more reasonable than to assume that the difference between men and women is "the missing clitoris"—in men.

If any one assumption is agreed on by the sex booklets it is the lamentable inferiority of the clitoris to the penis. As in the esthetics of Hollywood, size alone has been judged the primary esthetic attribute. It is the sheer size of the male organ that is supposed to impress little girls of five and six, producing an envy from which they never recover.

Has the clitoris any purpose at all? Neither its presence nor its happiness contributes to childbearing. It does not add directly to the pleasure of the man, something which cannot be said of the vagina. The Germans have called the clitoris *Wollustorgan*, the ecstasy organ; but it is more commonly frowned on as autoerotic, infantile (Freud), vestigial (like the tonsils) and in general the progenitor of no good. Marriage manuals, in their chapters on anatomy, admit grudgingly that this organ is the most sexually sensitive organ in the female body, capable of the most acute sensations. But toward the end of the same books, where recommendations are handed down, anatomy is subtly pushed into the background in order that women may be informed that the fullest expression of their sexual nature is not reached until sensation is felt as acutely in the vagina as in the clitoris.[1]

The clitoris, then, is not supposed to be as sensitive as the vagina, certainly not more sensitive. It shouldn't be, but it is.

The mystery of the clitoris, if one wishes to speak in mysteries, is its ability to accommodate the same quantity, as well as quality, of nerve endings that the penis accommodates. In the clitoris the multitudinous nerve endings are concentrated into an extremely small area, almost as small as an apple seed, while the same quantity of nerves are, in the penis, distributed over a much wider area.

"The female organ is minute compared with the male organ," writes Dr. Robert Latou Dickinson, "but the size of its nerves and the number of nerve endings in the glans of the clitoris compare strikingly with the same provision for the male. Indeed, Kobelt states that the glans of the clitoris is demonstrably richer in nerves than the male glans, for the two stems of the dorsalis clitoridis are relatively three to four times as large as the equivalent nerves of the penis. Without dividing up, they run mostly with three branches to the edge of the glans. Here, before their entry, they are so thick one can hardly comprehend how such a volume of nerve tissue can find room between the numberless blood-vessels of the tiny glans. Arrived near the surface of the glans they dispose themselves, just as in the male glans, in an intricate plexus, running also in loops into the tender membrane of the prepuce." [2]

It was quite a feat of nature to grant the small clitoris the same number of nerves as the penis. It was an even more incredible feat that society should actually have convinced the possessors of this organ that it was sexually inferior to the penis.

"The location of sensation in orgasm," writes Dr. Dickinson, "is vulvo-vaginal in the majority of women, but it is my guess that in one-third it is, under present conditions, chiefly or altogether on the outside, that is vulvar." [3] In his work, A Thousand Marriages, he states that women described the typical orgasm as an "ecstatic diffusion of sensation centered in the vulva. . . . There are not many accounts of exclusively vaginal orgasm, though the patient rather often says feeling is both vulvar and vaginal." [4]

The reflex of sexual excitement and orgasm is not as automatic, in either men or women, as some writers have maintained. Shame or unwillingness readily neutralize sensory pleasure, producing indifference or pain. A concentration of feminine shame, therefore, in the orgasm-producing area of the vulva, especially the clitoris, would offer some explanation for the widespread frigidity today. In most sexual behavior the stimulation of the vagina during intercourse communicates stimulus to the clitoris. However, all pleasure that befalls this organ runs into an overwhelming social censorship.

The experience of the clitoris is highly localized, staccato, demanding, and intense. The experience of the vagina, however intense it may be, is relatively more responsive, kinesthetic, and diffuse. Even this sensitivity of the vagina lies not in its upper portion, but in the small ring of tissue near the surface. The upper vagina has been termed "anesthetic" by gynecologists. Such lack of nerve

endings finds confirmation in the wide use of suppository methods in connection with menstruation.
Placed above the sensitive ring of tissue at the entrance of the vagina, the cotton suppository is not
felt.

If women testify to a strong sensation in the
upper portion of the vagina, it is their evidence and
no one else's that is relevant. But as Dickinson
writes, a consciousness for example of the impact of
semen "may be fanciful because the cervix [mouth
of womb] is like the upper vagina in being poorly
endowed with nerve endings." [5]

Because the sensitivity of the vagina has been
stressed to the exclusion of the vulva and clitoris,
the size of the penis has often been considered of
primary importance. But if this sensitivity continues
only an inch or two within the body, size of penis is
not as important as has been supposed.

Totem and Taboo

If the clitoris were allowed to act and react with
the full conviction of its nerve centers, the myth of
woman's diffuseness in sex might evaporate. Diffuseness is brought on by society's solemn insistence
that women concentrate entirely on the response of
the vagina, while relegating the sensations of the
clitoris over to the vaginal center. Whether this relegation, or banishment, is expected to be partial or
complete varies from writer to writer. Freud, in at
least one pronouncement, seems to favor complete
relegation.*

* "In the transition to womanhood very much depends upon
the early and complete relegation of this sensitivity from the

Any organ, large or small, which contains the multitude of nerve endings possessed by the clitoris is likely to be, in the lingo of physiologists, highly "irritable." Husbands frequently complain that the trouble with the clitoris is that it is too sensitive—when they are not complaining that it is not sensitive enough. Any organ with such a concentration of nerves will, when stimulated, find itself in an insistent frame of mind. While the vagina is more "responsive" than the clitoris, it may be that the clitoris is more "demanding" than the vagina.

A woman is supposed to respond, not insist or demand. She should put the needs of her husband first. To regard her own sexual needs as on a par with man's is to endanger the priority of the male impulse. Of course there is no reason why the total network of sensory nerves should not work in unison, and a concordance of impulses prevail. But in an imperfect world, what happens if they do not harmonize? Who is to submit to the will of the other? Clearly such subordination, rechristened adaptability, best fits the receptive nature of woman.

How Do You Pronounce It?

An organ that is so seldom pronounced at all, even in medical colleges, is bound to have difficulty establishing any standard pronunciation. Clitoris can be pronounced in almost any way, as long as the

---

clitoris over to the vaginal orifice. In those women who are sexually anaesthetic, as it is called, the clitoris has stubbornly retained this sensitivity." [6] This is a viewpoint which fits in with the frequent psychoanalytic belief that sensitivity of the clitoris is practically commensurate with sexual frigidity.

stress on the first syllable is retained. *Clítt-or-iss* is most common. *Cléet-or-iss* is occasional, but rare. The correct pronunciation, *Clíte-or-iss*, is employed only by Webster, who has really very little to do with family life or social organization.

Perhaps the persistent soft *i* that is popularly given this word can be traced to a subconscious desire on the part of scholars to reduce by phonetic magic the actual frequency of the organ! So dialectical a supposition is not unreasonable, since the soft vowel *i* is acoustically a sound of lower frequency than the strong vowel *i*. It is at least an amusing supposition.

Let us take a few examples from the realm of onomatopoeia, which has been amply studied by psychologists in recent years. A bird that *flits* has not nearly the emphasis of a bird in *flight*. A little *bit* does not shock us like a *bite*. A *fit* is more passive than a *fight*. And therefore a *clittoris* is likely to be much less of a problem than a *cliteoris* would be.

The word under discussion originated in Greek where it looked like this: κλειτορις. Translated into the letters of our alphabet it becomes, *kleitoris*. Now, a Greek formulation with *kleit-* in it always receives a strong vowel from scholars. It is significant that in this one word, however, the imperishable rules of scholarship gave way to a more irresistible psychological need: that of suppressing the pronunciatory gusto of an organ which never did quite fit in with woman's subordinate role in society. In this case, *kleit-* was obliged to adopt the more diffident and shy vowel, *i*.

The issue is clarified when we compare the phonetic encouragement given the male organ of generation. The Latin word here employed, commencing with *pen-*, was rendered into English with a strong vowel *e*. Now *pen-* is not the same as the Latin *poen-*, which takes a strong vowel, *e*, as in penal (Alcatraz). *Pen-* is like *penicillus*, which became the word *pencil*. In fact, *penicillus* was originally the diminutive of *penis*, suggesting that the latter should receive the soft vowel *e*. Could it be, we ask incredulously, that scholars, inventing a strong vowel for the male, at the same time deprived the homologous female structure of its classic emphasis?

When certain English verbs change from the present tense to the past, they replace their strong vowels with soft vowels, as befits an occurrence that is fading away into the misty distance. We bite in the present, but we bit in the past; we fight in the present, we fought in the past; we feed at the present and were fed in the past.

It is not unlikely that the mutation of *cliteoris* into *clittoris* has served to suggest to a gullible public that this organ, along with women's sexual satisfaction, has actually gone the way of the dinosaur. One likes to envisage the difficulty Freud might have run into if he had had to prove the universal existence of something called *pennis envy*. An organ with so undistinguished a title as this would have had difficulty commanding attention at all, much less earning the jealousy of little girls.

CHAPTER FIVE

love at bay

Sweet boy, she says, this night I'll waste in sorrow,
For my sick heart commands mine eyes to watch;
Tell me, love's master, shall we meet tomorrow,
Say, shall we, shall we, wilt thou make the match?
  He tells her no, tomorrow he intends
  To hunt the boar with certain of his friends.

SHAKESPEARE: *Venus and Adonis*

Venus, who was unaware that women are not by nature aggressive, here importunes the young Adonis. She is prepared to spend the night in sorrow, and asks only that on the morrow, "Say, shall we, shall we?" Sad to relate, Adonis had a previous engagement.

The enviable mood of preoccupation which men are able to get into, the profound air of something on the mind, of the business associate that must be phoned, the pipe that must be smoked or the baseball scores committed to memory: such things as these prompted John Donne to exclaim that love could admit the poor, the foul, the false to its pleasures, but not the busy man.

Man's diligence may reflect a commendable interest in the external world. On some occasions, however, his indifference to love appears to be an escape from sex itself as much as from the frills of romance. For a man who experiences a terror of personal intimacies will readily conceal his sense of guilt in a manly lust for activity and worldly conquest. It is no secret that women are not alone in their respect for modesty and convention. Husbands are as insistent on decorum and propriety as their wives. With taboos and conflicts raging within, a man may counteract sinful intimacies with his wife by a wide circulation among outside interests, and then counteract these philanderings in turn by a self-conscious adherence to family obligations.

The Frigid Wife and the Doting Mother

Men are raised by women, and their earliest acquaintance with the opposite sex is with that person whose relationship to them is maternal and protective. This person, the mother, is the first to bestow affection on the boy, and because her training stresses the maternal impulse above the sexual, she bestows a great deal of affection on her child, often withdrawing it rather conspicuously from her husband. It is significant that the same woman who awakens the boy's affection (and few deny the sexual component in all demonstrativeness) is also the first to issue the taboo against his sexuality. Mothers at one time or another inform their sons that it is naughty, or dangerous, or vile to handle their organs, to evince interest in others' organs, or to employ more than a perfunctory kiss within the family group.

Men are said to select women who in some wise resemble their mothers. Even if there is no outward resemblance, men may unconsciously associate their

wives with their mothers because their love relation
to human beings, and to members of the opposite
sex, stems from early contact with the mother.
While the deepest and warmest affection may have
been felt for the mother, and now is bestowed on
the wife, the man carries a profound conflict along
with this happy identity. The mother has, with
more or less hostile action, conveyed to the child
she bore that any more than a modified, and indeed
suppressed, love toward her will not be counte-
nanced.

The American mother is in most cases unable to
adopt anything approximating a conversational tone
on the question of sex. The little boy who is caught
handling his very interesting organs is generally
swooped upon by a mother with all claws spread; he
is punished and repudiated by the one being he
cares most for in all the world. Suppression of sexuality becomes the ticket to his mother's affection.

With the sharp shuttle of puritanism still running
through American life, those mothers who are affectionate and demonstrative toward their sons are
often neurotic and over-possessive as well. Their bitter struggle against frigidity or frustration has made
them over-dependent on their sons, and they refuse
to permit the transfer of time and affection to the
daughter-in-law. Loyalty to the mother forces the
son in this case to regard his wife unconsciously as
an interloper.

Many an American husband had as his mother a
woman unsatisfied sexually and reconciled to this
functional deprivation only by a philosophy somewhat antithetic to overt sex expression. She is, ordinarily, a woman deeply conscious of what other

people think, and while loving her son for himself, wants to have him measure up to the society which surrounds them. Society, for its part, approves of a young man who conceals his sexuality, and yet secretly requires perpetual sexual relief, a man who within marriage will without fuss nor prolongation expertly dispense his erotic impulses and bring forth young as a gesture of virility. In a very basic sense, a child is the only admission of marital eroticism that wins the approbation of society. Nowhere among these requirements is there a concern for the wife's satisfaction. And so another frigid wife and doting mother is in the making.

When the son learned to inhibit his love for his mother, he came to rely upon those inhibitions as the only milieu appropriate to a love object.[1] The mother has taught the son that overt sexual expression between man and woman is the most heinous of crimes, and often when a man adopts a wife, his conscience is salved only by perfunctoriness on his part supplemented by sexual indifference on hers. Occasionally men are shocked to learn that women are capable of an active sexual impulse. Erotic tendencies in a wife may be subconsciously rejected as unclean.

The Antisepsis, Beauty

The American boy's ideal is of a curiously lusty but non-physical love. His ideal woman is extraordinarily beautiful, and beauty itself signalizes a kind of purity. Purity is of value because it indicates that a woman is too pure and disinterested to make any sexual demands. Which is to say, she will wait until he is in the mood.

Many men are today living on a mirage as regards women. The ideal they seek is a pure fiction, a product of technological efficiency, of cinematic decor. She is a person to whom the photographers are kind in covering her mole or reducing her chin, to whom the scenario writers are generous in providing her with witty lines, to whom life is expedient in keeping her from actual contact with the admiring men.

Visitors to Hollywood come home with incredible news: that such and such an actress is fat, that another is not even pretty, that a third has eczema. American women are apt to smile to themselves when they hear this, for it helps to know that perfection is not even in Hollywood. But still the reproachful advertisements counsel them to make a further stab at pure and impenetrable beauty.

The ideal of woman as perfect in form and innocent in being is the antiseptic guard which men have erected against animal sex, not only against the woman's sex but against their own. Since everyone owns imperfections of one sort or another, there is no better way to dehydrate the sexuality of a woman and fix the residue as a pure and reliable love object than to evolve an ideal with no imperfection of any kind. With a reasonable facsimile of the ideal he finds touted in the movies, the American male believes he could really let himself go, really have that "perfect sex life," sans irritation or satiation. If this man has a wife, he puts up with her deviations from the ideal as best he can (yes, and she puts up with his); but he tends to preserve his ideal—at least for Saturday nights at the movies.

Turning to the most sophisticated stereotype of all, we find the ideal is of a distant, virginal, haughty, warm-eyed woman. High heels, fitted dress, fortress of fur, small perishable hat, and above all the wet signal of lipstick, the sweatless drift of powder, the dark highlighting of the eyes. One can discern the thread of a minority mandate in the requirement that the nose be small (otherwise it is aggressive), the eyes large (a receptive character), and the mouth just right (it should not look as though it could talk). This woman, while positively littered with symbols of sexuality, promises to be inaccessible to any thoughts carnal, rational or humanistic. It is possible that men, in some cases, find this impregnability reassuring.

The ideals of feminine beauty are enough to abash most of us. Yet man's attempt to clean up the business of sex did not stop here. For ancient and modern man played his trump card in the dehydration of women's sexuality by giving woman a deep sense of shame concerning her bodily functions. When in recent years the untouchableness of the lower caste was commuted into a "scientific account" of wastes and foul odors *versus* natural feminine daintiness, American industry and a sex-frightened world joined hands.

The purification of sex is fast becoming the virtual eradication of sex, while the small voices of protesting gynecologists are scarcely heard amid the drug-store welter of fumigators especially designed for the female of the species.

Lady Macbeth might signalize for modern woman the heart of all terror, the guilty conviction that feminine daintiness is being jeopardized. *Out, damned spot! out, I say!* cries Lady Macbeth. *What, will these hands ne'er be clean? Here's the smell of*

*the blood still: all the perfumes of Arabia will not
sweeten this little hand. Oh! oh! oh!* And her injunction, *Wash your hands, put on your nightgown,*
might serve as a motto for the romantic antisepsis of
American nuptial regulations.

Is it true that women's bodies are naturally less
tidy than men's? Is it correct that the secretions of
the female are more objectionable than the analogous secretions of the male? While advertisements,
it can be expected, exploit the ignorance and puritanism of the public, physicians themselves sometimes reveal a subtle conviction that women's
glands are a little less civilized than men's.[2]

Cleanliness is to be distinguished from non-clean-
liness, but is time to call a halt to the hygiene
anxiety tormenting America. We have nightmares
of drowning in a sea of Listerine and Lysol with
nothing but bars of Lifebuoy to which to cling.
The motivation behind this is a preposterous sexual
fastidiousness which has selected women as its lu-
crative scapegoat. Women are expected to carry the
purity tradition for the entire race of mankind, leaving men free to enjoy themselves in the dirty work
of war, politics, business, and animal satisfaction.
Since sexual passion is apt, physiologically, to produce secretions, the prudent woman would do well
to maintain a strict sexual frigidity lest John change
toward her, having discovered she is something more
than his mother.

Two Sides of the Coin

A distinction is generally made between impotence and frigidity. Since only the male is supposed

to act or be potent, it has seemed reasonable to describe his inability or unwillingness to act as *impotence*. On the other hand, a woman's native passivity simply froze over in extreme cases, and became frigidity.

In both impotence and frigidity, however, similar conditions prevail: the erectile tissue fails to reply to stimuli and orgasm is absent. If the sex act is redefined in a way that includes the participation of the woman, a lack of actability in her could be called impotence, a lack of responsiveness in the man, frigidity.

Male frigidity functions in an elaborate inhibition of caress and a lack of psychological flexibility. If man's attitude toward caress were merely one of indifference, one might consider the possibility of his epidermis being impenetrable to anything short of a pin-prick or an ice-sensation. Some experiments have actually attempted to come up with this, but their results are less than convincing.

The unhappy and conventional woman usually struggles to become more diffuse in her sex experience, as the books tell her she should be; the result may be impotence locally and frigidity emotionally. A man may struggle to become totally local in his experience, since this is supposed normal for men, with the result that a self-conscious impotence develops locally and a mental frigidity generally.

Impotence as local passivity, and frigidity as psychological deadlock, are so closely related in human sex experience that it seems unwise to view them as a simple dichotomy parceled out to the male and the female respectively.

CHAPTER SIX

witchcraft and
the moon

*In the beginning, said a Persian poet, Allah took
a rose, a lily, a dove, a serpent, a little honey, a
Dead Sea apple, and a handful of clay. When he
looked at the amalgam—it was a woman.*

WILLIAM SHARP

When men write books on women, they generally
invoke a being called Nature: a ministering angel
who apparently has little to do with insects,
droughts or epidemics, but who exists solely to see
that women cultivate all those little charms considered appropriate to them.

When these same writers approach the natural
functions of women which do not directly answer to
the needs of men, their old friend Nature is likely to
drop out of the account entirely, or put on a face
more appropriate to the Grim Reaper. Menstruation and the menopause cannot by any stretch of
masculine logic be regarded as evolution's answer to
man's immediate pleasure. These two natural phenomena have therefore assumed an exaggerated role
of tragedy in sex literature.

When Time Is at Its Period

*And if a woman have an issue, and her issue in
her flesh be blood, she shall be put apart seven days:
and whosoever toucheth her shall be unclean until
the even.* Primitive tribes frequently isolate the
menstruating woman in a hut at the outskirts of the
village. She is a witch who can contaminate any
man she catches sight of.

In early phases of history when death and the
shedding of blood were surrounded with superstition, woman's ability to shed blood at certain regular intervals may well have inspired awe in the
hunters and warriors of the time. Perhaps they ritu-
alistically transferred their fear of death to women:
all the more satisfactorily since the woman eventually recovered (as the dead warrior did not)
and became a desirable sex object once more. Perhaps the uncleanliness ritual also taught women a
lesson, demonstrating that they escaped total
ostracism by only the closest margin.

Is menstrual blood poisonous? It is as though
man were anxious to document his conditioned horror of the affair, and if science would only oblige
with some small fact, such as the poisonousness of
the blood, he could relax in the vise of inherited
prejudice. Unfortunately it is not poisonous. It does
contain thirty times as much lime as ordinary blood,
but this does not explain the intolerant attitude
toward it.

Arterial blood is pure, venous blood is waste
blood. The latter is carried to the lungs where it is
purified by the exchange of carbon dioxide for oxy-
gen. The sweet breath of one's beloved, inciden-

tally, is nothing more than a small dose of lethal gas. Menstrual blood, emerging from small capillaries, is not venous blood. Since it is a concomitant of the preparation the uterus has made for the young and helpless embryo, poisonous blood would be a very poor nutritional milieu to provide.

Menstruation is not an illness but a sign of the continued health of ovaries and uterus, and of the smooth functioning of the sex hormones. Physical exercise is often of positive benefit, probably because it relaxes muscular tensions. Variations of a few days in the cycle are the usual experience. A flow of four days means a loss of less than two ounces of blood.

Menstruation is controlled by the positive action of hormones supplied by the pituitary gland. The pituitary gland resides in the head, in close proximity to the magnificent structure of the human brain, which alone should give the process a dignity. Nor are lower animals capable of menstruation, for only a few of the higher apes share this distinction.

Many sex manuals intimate that intercourse during menstruation is not cricket. Few volumes resist a hint of unhealthiness or danger. Writes Dr. I. E. Hutton, "Intercourse should not take place during the period for reasons, chiefly esthetic, which will be obvious." These mysterious extra-esthetic reasons are never specified. Instead it is added that if intercourse "inadvertently" takes place, "there is no possibility whatever of harmful effects." [1]

Thus intercourse during menstruation is without harm, but society places an esthetic taboo on it. The rigidity of this custom has contributed to a resentment by women which may permeate their sexual relationship at other times. The notion that orgasm is impossible during menstruation is incorrect.

It may be added that some rare cases of sterility were cured by the discovery that the particular women were fertile only during menstruation. Told to disregard their scruples, all conceived successfully.[2]

Confusion among the Patriarchs

Writers on sex have never been able to decide whether sexual feeling is at its minimum or at its maximum around menstruation. Two treatises, Dr. Fritz Kahn's *Our Sex Life* and Dr. Kenneth Walker's *The Physiology of Sex*, labor opposite views.

According to Dr. Kahn, menstruation is a time of non-sexuality. "The woman's sexual character resembles the cycle of the moon: it changes rhythmically every four weeks from the zero point of the new moon [menstruation] to the full moon during the middle of the month [ovulation]." [3]

This he contrasts with the sexuality of the male: "The sex life of a man resembles the course of the sun: it shines regularly at all times and at all seasons." It occurs to us to wonder just where this remarkable climate has been hiding itself—where the sun, the male sexuality, shines at all times and at all seasons, uninhibited by snow, sleet, or the necessity of setting.

If women experience a depressed sexuality during menstruation, as Dr. Kahn asserts, it hardly seems surprising. For centuries women were isolated at this time, for further centuries permitted in the house but pronounced sexually untouchable for a fifth of each month. It would be no surprise if shame took over their thoughts at these periods and drove out other considerations.

Dr. Kenneth Walker takes a considerably different stand, maintaining that there is a peak in sexual desire about the time of menstruation. "Just as it is during the 'oestrus,' or heat, that the female animal allows the approach of the male, so in a woman the period of maximum desire generally falls somewhere about the time of menstruation."* [4]

But oestrus in animals is the time of ovulation, of the production of the egg and the peak of fertility. Ovulation occurs in women; it is likewise the time of production of the egg and the peak of fertility. If heat or sexual need actually centers around the time of menstruation rather than at ovulation (approximately thirteen days after menstruation), it is less an indication of nature's wisdom than of her misapprehension.

However, we think far better of nature than this. While the testimony of thousands of women has placed the period of maximum desire in the vicinity of menstruation and not at ovulation, various factors may be influencing this testimony and in a real sense distorting it. The subject is important enough to venture a few hypotheses.

* The confusion of oestrus and menstruation often gains credence because of the show of blood in some of the lower animals at the time of heat. This, however, is caused by changes which the vagina undergoes as a preparation for heat, while menstruation is due to changes in the uterus which prepare it for implantation. Menstruation does not occur in lower animals such as the dog.

"Oestrus" Comes from the Latin Gadfly

Emotions around the time of menstruation differ in different women and also for the same woman at different times. Suppose, however, we assume that one type of sexual desire may prove more dominant at the time of menstruation, and another type of desire at ovulation.* These periods are at opposite points in the cycle, being thirteen or fourteen days apart. Before menstruation the uterus prepares itself for a potential embryo. This preparation involves the multiplication of blood vessels, the accumulation of blood, and therefore moderate congestion of the tissues. Processes in the uterus build up special tissues for the nourishment of the fertilized ovum.

Mild nervousness or sluggishness sometimes is present at this time, though there is no rule about this. Women often mention sensitivity of tissues. If the emotions at this time are at all distinguishable from those at other phases of the cycle, one would expect that they might be marked by receptivity, a love characterized by tenderness and dependence, and some hint of maternalism.

Suppose the human female undergoes an oestral period as well as a menstrual one. Oestrus would involve a flurry of sexual desire occurring about the time of ovulation. Without putting too much stress on oestrus as *frenzy*, its classic equivalent, one

* To postulate a possible *influence* of menstrual cycle on the fluctuations of desire is not to suggest that the cycle is the sole or even primary cause of sexual desire. There are innumerable associated factors, glandular, psychological, and circumstantial, which may prove more significant at a given time.

would yet expect that the action of hormones just before maximum fertility might induce in women a dim sort of agitation.

In other words, the action of oestral hormones would induce a more *propulsive* sexual mood, rather than the relatively receptive and dependent mood at menstruation. The sex impulse does not originate in the sensitivity of surface tissues alone, but arises from the organism as a whole, since hormonic action informs the entire system. In all other animals this voice from within announces the spectacular arrival of a fertile ovum. This is oestrus or heat.

What would society think of this differential pattern of emotion—receptive, then propulsive—*if* it existed; and it is not known whether it exists or not. Society (and here hypothesis can become statement) would give resounding approval to the receptive type of desire, and taboo without hesitation the propulsive impulse. When a woman loves her husband with tenderness, gratitude, dependence, and maternalism, society finds her truly feminine. If, therefore, a spontaneous and propulsive sex drive occurred around the time of ovulation, few women would admit it, even to themselves.

Unless such a hypothesis is forwarded, suggesting the possible existence of sexual intensity around ovulation, it will be impossible to discover whether such a peak of intensity exists. In this connection, a remark of Dr. Dickinson's is of interest. "It is important negative evidence," he writes, "that orgasm is so seldom voluntarily mentioned as coming most easily in the vicinity of the menstrual period, although heightened sexual desire is thus associated." [5]

It may be that women suppress sexual desires except where these desires assume the receptive and moderate form approved by society.

It also may be that menstruation has served in past questionnaires on the subject as an all-too-convenient peg on which to hang all major events of women's physical life. Public events are often characterized as pre-war, duration, and post-war. Many women regard menstruation as the leading event of the cycle. Personal events then readily fall into either a pre- or post-menstrual period. Two weeks of pre-menstrual and two weeks of post-menstrual account for the entire month.

If women know that ovulation is occurring at the middle point of each month, this may become a second event around which to orient time. Only then will answers to questionnaires distinguish accurately the first week following menstruation from the second week, which is properly pre-ovulatory rather than post-menstrual.

what shall we do with the climacteric?

"There you have women," put in M. de Rênal,
*with a coarse laugh. "There's always something
out of order in their machinery."*
STENDHAL: *The Red and the Black*

Since men feel uneasy about the menstrual season,
one would suppose they would welcome the end of
menses or climacteric in women. This is not the
case. For no sooner has menstruation subsided than
the female glands and emotions begin (according to
tradition) to atrophy or wither in a shocking manner. This apparition of a decaying organism is not
something that enhances a woman's value.

Fortunately (according to tradition) nature provides that as woman's beauty fades, her sexual
feelings also fade. As the ovaries atrophy, the sexual
impulse passes into extinction. Mother love
emerges, uncomplicated by sexual love, and promotes the portrait we find in candy stores early in
May, a sort of gray-haired personification of the mol-
lifying impulse. The menopause, guaranteed to take
the briskness out of a woman, is "a period that calls
for conservation of energy," writes an authority on
marriage. "There is a gradual atrophy of physical

structure which puts an end to reproduction and eventually to sex experience." [1]

What are the elementary facts behind the climacteric? The one ovum or egg which customarily emerged from an ovary each month no longer puts in an appearance. Ordinarily the uterus prepared itself for implantation and, later, the menstrual flow began if implantation had not taken place. After the menopause the ovum does not emerge, the uterus does not prepare, and there is no consequent flow. The function of egg-production by the ovaries is discontinued.

This discontinuance is the rarest good luck for women. It is not that any great effort is required to produce the egg, or to have it fertilized, but that the gestation of the child is a strain that only the younger body is equipped to handle. Thus around fifty the woman is insured against further childbearing. In the ovaries at birth reside a multitude of potential eggs. At menopause these are literally used up.

Men continue to manufacture sperm throughout life. It is therefore supposed that their capacity to fertilize remains constant unto the eightieth year. However, capacity for erection does not indicate fertilizing capacity. Far fewer men are capable of fertilization in later years than is supposed. The production of viable sperm, as one physical process among many, usually undergoes reduction.

Men's ability to fertilize ova several years after women of the same age have no ova left to fertilize does not indicate that the male physique is more resistant to age. If men had not only to contribute the fertilizing sperm, but also to nurture the growing embryo within their bodies, there would undoubtedly be a discontinuance of sperm-production at forty-five or fifty. As it is, man has merely to contribute the sperm-cell.

Wives are customarily younger than their husbands and cease menstruating around forty-nine. It is impossible to say therefore how many men are functionally sterile at this time, since their fertilizing ability is not being tested.

Did You Say Conservation?

The psychological crisis of the menopause is granted by all to be far in excess of its physiological discomfort. Are women of fifty mourning their inability to bear more children? This is unlikely. Rather have women been told that sexual emotion is dependent on something called *youth*, which is equated with the menstrual cycle. When the cycle ceases, and the ovaries "atrophy," the sexual emotions are expected to grow cold as a dying star. It is this implication that promotes panic at menopause.

Literature on sex does not always state that sexual feeling is on a downhill course after menopause. It merely counsels the husband to be particularly patient and considerate of his climacterical spouse. In this, as in so many fields, theorists become so busy explaining the reasons behind a fact that they don't look to see if the fact is really there. Physicians are so preoccupied with explaining the reasons for the disappearance of sexual feeling in women of fifty that not many of them have stopped to ask: "By the way, madam, sexual feeling *has* disappeared, hasn't it?"

Dr. Dickinson did ask this question. He asked not only his younger patients but his post-menopause patients about their sexual desires. The older women compared their emotions with those they had had at the age of twenty, thirty, forty, and so on. According to these data, plotted on a chart, the woman's greatest peak of intensity of sexual desire was seen to come *during the climacteric*.[2]

At forty-four to fifty, when the booklets counsel conservation of energy, the administration of bromides, restraint and patience, wives candidly admit to an upsurge of emotion. Sexual irritability is better tranquilized by expression than by repression. Yet at the menopause a husband often curtails sexual relations entirely, begs his wife to have breakfast in bed, and worst of all, professes an eternal love for her spirit no matter how withered her ovaries become.

The women in Dickinson's study not only noted a rise in passion at the menopause, but a rise that outdistanced all previous peaks. They apparently desire as passionate a relationship at forty-five or fifty as at any other time of their life. It is at this juncture that the husband tiptoes in with a tray of soft-boiled eggs and a pot of Sanka.

We are not prepared to say this concentration of sexual desire at age forty-nine represents a primitive peak which can be checked by a comparative study of rabbits or chimpanzees. It is undoubtedly a characteristic of the human female only, and perhaps only of the upper-income group that comprised Dickinson's study. Possibly the woman's desire is augmented by the fear of losing desire. Or the removal of fears of excessive child-bearing may intensify her feelings. Possibly the mature woman recognizes for the first time her own sexual impulse as a spontaneous factor in her life.

Whatever the reasons for this peak in sexual desire, it remains a fact within this particular group of women. The evidence is sufficiently conclusive to impel us to reconsider some of the attendant facts of the climacteric. If women feel an intensity of passion at this time and physicians call for a conservation of energy, one can understand why psychological anxieties may develop.

The woman is not supposed to feel sexual, but she does. The fear of abnormality that haunted her childhood begins to plague her again. Child-bearing is over, and with it her sexual usefulness. What is it in her body that retains its original appetites? Why can't the sexual organs atrophy as they are supposed to? Sometimes she looks about at her friends who seem (she is probably mistaken) at peace with approaching age. Atrophy seems in them to be proceeding on schedule. And suddenly the woman feels like screaming.

Women do scream during the menopause. Who can blame them? Tradition insists that their emotions atrophy at the stroke of midnight, that henceforward no one can find them physically attractive. But they notice their emotions surging up wonderfully, and they do feel physically attractive. Can it be a dream? Are they deluded? Is this the madness of involution one hears about?

The groundwork is laid for a magnificent anxiety neurosis, of which women take full advantage. But the spadework in this anxiety neurosis has been accomplished (we regret to call names) by purity-

hounded, impotence-harried, mother-magnetized
men, who communicate to their wives their own ignorance of elementary biological fact. It is not true
that women need kindness at the menopause. They
need science.

First, the Facts

Both the female ovaries and the males testes are
composed of a variety of tissues. In the ovary one
type of tissue produces the eggs, which mature one
by one and are released each month into the fallopian tube. An equally important function of the female ovaries is the production of sex hormones
which circulate through the blood stream. After menopause, the egg-production function of the ovaries
ceases, but the ovaries continue their function of se-
creting sex hormones. They remain living glands,
they remain intact, they continue to function. To
speak of the atrophy of the ovaries is therefore not
only unsavory but unscientific.

Do sex hormones cease after menopause? They
do not. In both male and female the secretions of
the body as a whole slow up gradually with the advance of age, differing among individuals. Since the
secretion of sex hormones is one secretion among
others, they too lessen in some degree. But what
holds for the lessening of hormones in the female
holds for the male as well.

In men the production of sperm (spermatogen-
esis) does not, so far as is known, cease abruptly at
any given age. Yet those tissues in the testes which
produce sperm will function with diminished effort
—producing, therefore, fewer sperm and sperm that

are less apt and efficient in reproduction. No one knows to what extent the man of fifty is sterile. And only because sterility and impotence are so often confused has it seemed important to men that their fertility remain unquestioned unto the grave.

No complicated laboratory investigation of a woman's fertility is needed after menopause; it is clear that she cannot bear young. Men, by declining an investigation of their own fertility—an analysis of the semen—effectively prevent any generalization about themselves or the percentage in whom fertility has ceased at fifty or sixty.

After menopause the tissues of the ovary which produced the egg no longer function. But one of the most obscure chapters of endocrinology is the influence of egg-production on sexual emotion. The sex hormones, which we hear most about, come from an entirely different portion of the ovaries, a part that continues to function. If a man's testes are X-rayed, the sperm-producing tissues can be completely destroyed. But the interstitial cells of the testes will continue to manufacture hormones without hindrance. Sexual desire can be as intense as ever, even though the semen no longer carries any active sperm.

A woman's ovaries develop from the same tissues in the embryo that the male testes do. X-ray can destroy the egg-producing function of the ovaries, but it has no effect on the interstitial cells which continue to release hormones. The woman is sterile, but her sexual desire may be as intense as ever. Even in the ovariectomized woman the sex impulse continues. The immediate effect of removal of the ovaries may be hormone insufficiency, but in time the pituitary gland acts as a substitute in providing sex hormones. The sex impulse is not the function of one isolated gland, but a function of the whole organism.

Evolution cleverly distributed the source of the sex impulse through the body. It has hidden emotion away. Perhaps it was anticipated that the excision of the sex impulse would some day become one of the more absorbing occupations of medical science. Less than a hundred years ago there was a systematic attempt to track down the sex impulse to one organic structure after another, with a view to amputating it once and for all. Surgeons experimentally removed the ovaries of erotic women, and were disturbed to find that the sex impulse remained.

Another factor explains the continuation of sexual interest after menopause. The sensory nerves of the body do not, after all, atrophy at fifty. If they did, major operations could be performed without anesthetic after that time. But pleasure and pain persist. We admit that pain continues. Why do we deny the survival of pleasure?

Practical assistance for a civilized climacteric is offered in the use of ovarian extract. A simple operation can also be performed on the vagina if it has become expanded through child-bearing or muscular laxness.

Does the Maternal Instinct
Replace the Sexual?

Since women testify to a continuation of the sex impulse, and since the physiological factors that contribute to sexuality continue, why is it that

women as well as men have a fixed belief that the
sex impulse ought to wither? This dogma is con-
structed from several erroneous assumptions already
discussed:

*That woman's main source of sexual pleasure is
within her.* While the nerves of clitoris, vulva, and
vagina do not alter at menopause, the changes in
the uterus and ovaries are said to be what really
matter. If the womb is the "ideal" center around
which the sexuality of women is oriented, the total
loss of function suffered by the uterus at menopause
should have an extinguishing influence on the entire
sex life.

*That woman's sexuality is wholly dependent on
stimulus from her menstrual cycle.* When the cycle
ends, and sexuality no longer knows what to fluc-
tuate with, it stops.

*That woman's charm lies in her beauty, purity,
and receptivity.* After menopause her charm lies in
her purity and receptivity, with sweet motherliness
compensating for loss of beauty.

That the wife is ideally the mother. The fastidi-
ous husband who has identified his wife with his
mother may look forward to his wife's becoming
older, perhaps resembling his mother therefore; but
expects her to become less and less sexual. She now
becomes "the mother of his children." A woman of
fifty has no *reason* to wish satisfaction, while a husband must be free to rove, due to natural and inher-
ent factors.

Only when the climax of woman's erotic experience is identified with the specific function of
child-bearing can the end of child-bearing, or menopause, be expected to lessen erotic interest.

The linking of child-bearing and sexuality has a
consequence for more than the woman entering menopause. Millions of women for whom child-bearing
has not been possible suffer from this superstition.
There are the marriages of Rh positive men and Rh
negative women, in whom the probability of offspring is seriously reduced. There are other women
who through physical accidents, small pelvises
(often due to rickets), closed fallopian tubes, or the
sterility of the husband will never be able to bear
children.[3] Are these women to believe that sexual
gratification is impossible for them?

The sexual potential of a given woman depends
entirely on her individual emotions, desires, and
capacity for satisfaction. If her desire for children is
frustrated, it is a serious but separate matter. Her
sexual desires are not dependent on the size of her
pelvis or the presence or absence of an Rh factor in
the blood.

Recent trends in psychoanalysis have especially
contributed to this notion of the indivisibility of the
maternal and the sexual instinct. Woman's envy of
the penis is said to be compensated for by man's
envy of child-bearing. Psychoanalysis, however, has
also stressed the desire to return to the womb. How
are we to know when the male is envying the child-
bearing woman and when he is merely envying the
happy security of the child?

Many of the more eloquent paeans to motherhood have a narcissistic ring—almost as though men
were congratulating their own mothers for having
had the good fortune to bear them. The average
man, and perhaps the analyst, may like the idea that
the maternal instinct replaces the sexual because it

means that at the moment of the son's birth, the mother renounces the father once and for all. Maternity supplants sexuality, and mother is no longer the sexual companion of father, but the pure and selfless guardian of her son. Could any better pipe dream be invented by the Oedipus complex?

The Manly Illusion

Since sexual satisfaction is so often identified with child-bearing, it is no surprise that sterility is often blamed on sexual frigidity, and frigidity on sterility. This myth is best dissipated by discussing its masculine counterpart: that sterility and impotence are interchangeable. Impotence brings functional sterility because viable sperm, even if present in the testes, are not released. But the reverse is not true. There can be an absence of fertilizing sperm accompanied by vigor and potency. The reflex of erection is not dependent upon the presence of fertile spermatozoa.

Confusion of fertility and virility is, however, often comforting. It suggests that a man's fertility is tested merely by erection. This assumption has its adverse effect on women, for it has meant that an infertile marriage is automatically blamed on the woman.

Dr. George Gellhorn as far back as 1924 stated that "all modern observers, with rare unanimity of opinion, agree that in fully half of the cases the cause of the sterile marriage must be sought in the man." [4] Unfortunately science cannot, with one succinct statement of fact, dissipate a superstition so deeply ingrained in the fabric of society. Few readers turn to the *Gynecological and Obstetrical Monographs* for information. In his popular treatise, Dr. Kahn writes similarly: "It is generally popular to put the blame for the sterility of a marriage on the woman, but this is completely senseless as long as the fertility of the man is not proved." [5]

After this generous beginning, inclination proves too strong, however, and the total impression of Dr. Kahn's chapter on sterility is to again place the major blame at the door of woman. One notes a special unwillingness to suggest that male sterility can be due to a mal*functioning.* Female trouble has been such a favorite joke with men that it would be painful to admit how often a man's trips to the urologist are prompted by aches and pains inhabiting the sex organs. And social insistence on virility has prevented men from deriving quite the satisfaction from invalidism that women do. Perhaps that is one reason his death rate exceeds hers.

Since the urinary and genital tracts are so closely knit in the male, the urologist has with euphemistic camouflage taken over the treatment of man's prostatic, testicular, and vesicular disabilities, while the female public remains persuaded that this specialist treats solely the bladder. There has been no camouflage of the existence of the gynecologist. That a full-time specialist is required for women's ills is known to all.

Dr. Kahn lists four causes of sterility in the male: *impotence* (his cross-reference stresses primarily the failure of wives to be attractive or stimulating); *premature ejaculation* (over-excitement or fear or abhorrence of women); *former inflammations of the testicles and of the epididymis, usually as a result* of gonorrhea (cross-reference mentions gonorrhea, caught from a woman; other causes of inflammation are ignored). The fourth reason for male sterility is probably the most important: *congenital inferiority of the semen (lack of sperm cells; few sperm cells; lack of motility in the sperm cells, etc.)*.

The word *congenital* is added apparently to suggest that inferiority of the semen is present from birth (maybe the fault of the mother?). A man doesn't like to think his system is capable of developing the engine trouble he finds so amusing in the physiology of women. This fourth reason for sterility could well have been discussed under a multitude of headings. The inadequacy of the semen, its inability to stand body temperature, the malfunctioning of its secretions, and so on, are complex and as Dr. Kahn has said of feminine hygiene require "a large chapter." The causes of male sterility are nevertheless crowded into four cryptic items and one paragraph, while the remaining twelve pages of this chapter are reserved for discussion of the causes of sterility in women.

These causes include factors for which the female is scarcely to be held uniquely responsible, such as unsuitable positions during intercourse and a biological lack of harmony between sperm and egg. In place of a *lack* of sperm cells, one finds in the female a *failure* to produce eggs. In place of the dignified *congenital* difficulties of the male, one finds something called *infantilism* causing widespread sterility in women. Infantilism, it turns out, means anything from a narrow pelvis to undeveloped ovaries. If the term sounds more akin to a sexual perversion than a physical condition, the reader

is not far wrong. For the wide incidence of infantilism is attributed to the decline of the ideal of beauty,
a lack of discrimination in choice of marriage part-
ners, our unnatural modes of life, late marriages,
antagonistic attitudes toward sex.[6]

Testing for Fertility

It is not always easy to determine who is chiefly
responsible for sterility. A highly hospitable reception for relatively weak sperm may insure fertilization, while an inhospitable reception of highly viable sperm may discourage fertilization. Whether in a
given case the sperm should be strong enough to
withstand an unusual acidity in the vagina, or
whether the vagina should be alkaline enough to
make it easier for weak sperm to survive—this is an
endless debate. In all such debates of the past, men
have been given the benefit of the doubt.

In 1939, at the very brink of the atomic age, a
physician in a leading medical journal complained
that doctors in testing the fertility of male sperm
were occasionally doing so under conditions that
had little to do with the circumstances of human reproduction. Sperm prefer cool temperatures. If kept
at a sub-room-temperature they can exhibit a great
deal of compulsive activity and sexual élan, which
may or may not be present in real life. Thus a sam-
ple of semen, kept cool enough, will go through fire
and water, remain immune to deadly acids, propel
itself with relentless initiative, and in general make
one grandstand play after another. We can imagine
how pleased a worried husband is to hear about this.

Yet as Dr. Abner I. Weisman suggests, "spermato-

zoa in the course of their physiologic wanderings inside of the female never or rarely encounter lower
temperatures than 37° C. . . . Therefore to study
motility, reaction to acidity, etc., of human spermatozoa at 8 to 20° C. or at room temperatures is . . .
comparable to studying the sex life of an Eskimo
while in the tropics." [7]

Are sperm being tested for their ability to participate in normal reproduction, or for the pleasure of
seeing them display maximum motility under artifi-
cial conditions? This type of proof serves admirably
to transfer blame to the woman. Even "the finding
of a few viable spermatozoa does not indicate a
semen of fecundating vigor," write Doctors Cary
and Dickinson;[8] for there is a high death toll among
sperm during the hazardous journey toward the egg.

The Climacterical Male

In Dickinson's study of intensity of desire, the
women's peak was between forty-four and fifty,
while men testified to a peak around thirty-five.
That men frequently do experience an excitement
at the age of forty or thereabouts is generally acknowledged. What is more important, no one thinks
of depriving them of it.

Are women more melancholic than men at the
approach of age? Who can be sure? Women, under
constant surveillance by husband and children, have
every irritability noted. Men find outlets for dissatisfaction at the office and in all their activities outside
the home.

If it is common for a young man to fear impotence, it is likely that some men encounter middle

age with foreboding. Husbands may occasionally be anxious to believe their wives sexless for fear they themselves will prove inadequate. As a sedative for impending hysteria, man's use of alcohol is quite as widespread as women's resort to the triple bromide. While no one looks into the reasons why one man and another craves his nightcap, everyone knows why women take bromides: they are the lost sex.

A slowing down of physical processes occurs in both male and female. This can in each case be called change of life. If Promethean man, however, should find himself in the same climacterical boat as his wife, we would hear far less about the atrophy of the ovaries and the cessation of the sex impulse. Men who consider "ovarian insufficiency" an objective and noncommittal phrase would think differently if "testicular insufficiency" became common.

society writes biology

well) here's looking at ourselves
E. E. CUMMINGS

There is a prevalent belief that scientists are unprejudiced. It is true that they of all citizens make the most stirring attempt at objectivity, but in realms close to the social structure, as in the biological sciences, it is easy for the scientist and popularizer of science to slip into hidden evaluations in their reports on organic fact. If we like their bias, we contentedly ignore it. In accounts of sexual processes, however, there is a painfully persistent tendency to award the female a derogatory role.

By capturing the mood, and an occasional phrase, from various widely selling sex books, we shall piece together a typical account entitled *A Patriarchal Society Writes Biology*. The outstanding device for entering opinion under the guise of objective fact, we will see, is consistently to animate one portion of a process and *de*-animate the other. The male cell acts, voluntarily, yet with a teleological sense of destiny, while the female reacts, involuntarily, taking her cues from him.

For in the patriarchal account, the male sperm is by all odds the central character. We watch his actions with breathless suspense. He is an independent little creature, single-minded, manly, full of charm, resourcefulness and enterprise, who will make his own minute decision to swim toward the egg.

The female egg is portrayed as the blushing bride, ignorant but desirable, who awaits arousal by the gallant male cell. The egg, like the human female, is receptive. In most accounts of the physiology of sex, the writer becomes rhapsodic over the relaxed and nutritious condition of the waiting ovum. Since the egg is not known to be capable of self-motion, it is regarded as helpless.

The sperm is the purposeful agent in reproduction; the egg learns direction and purpose only after union with the sperm. Thus the human ovum is a country cousin until entered by the worldly male cell; the human female is only half alive until she is pregnant.

In choice of terms the patriarchal biologist makes liberal use of the word *vestigial*, as applied to any organ in the female which is similar to an organ in the male but not quite like it. The uterus escapes being called a vestigial prostate because it bears sons, but the clitoris has never thrown off the label of vestigial penis.

The patriarchal biologist employs *erection* in regard to male organs and *congestion* for female. Erection of tissue is equivalent to the filling of the local blood vessels, or congestion; but erection is too aggressive-sounding for women. Congestion, being associated with the rushing of blood to areas that have been infected or injured, appears to scientists to be a more adequate characterization of female response.

While robbing us of some of our illusions about

father science, the discussion may have a salutary effect upon poets, who have expressed fears that the language was losing its flavor and its myth-creating qualities. Opinions are still hiding out among us, but less often in such naïve adjectives as *good* and *bad*, *superior* and *inferior*. Opinion finds just as adequate shelter, and a wider market, by adopting the dress of the times—the lingo of Science, its vocabulary and its accent.

A Patriarchal Society Writes Biology

EMBRYOLOGY

Male. The human embryo first passes through an indifferent or asexual stage in which it is not possible to distinguish male from female. In the second month, however, nature prepares for the great differentiation which is to come.

The genital projection, later the penis, is joined by a large genital fold, a sort of collar. This collar later becomes the scrotum.

Along the genital projection is a cleft, a median slit which leads to the kidneys and internal genital glands.

As development proceeds, the penis grows rapidly, and the genital cleft closes to form the urethra which opens temporarily at the base of the glans.

In the third month the glans splits and forms a groove which recloses, continuing the urethra to its proper place at the tip of the penis.

Just before or after birth the testes progress from their position within the pelvic region to their definitive place in the scrotum.

Thus the male human being has utilized the asex-

ual embryonic projection (or genital tubercle) to
develop the organs of penis and scrotum.

Female. The female, we find, does not develop in
any important way from the asexual or early embryonic state. Her sexual organs remain in an infantile
condition, displaying an early arrest of development.

Whereas in the male the genital tubercle progresses rapidly toward the mature penis form, the
genital tubercle in the female embryo slowly re-
gresses until it forms the clitoris, or vestigial penis, a
minute glans hidden in an upper depression of the
vulva.

Similarly, the genital cleft which successfully
closes in the male remains as a pronounced un-
sealed slit in the female, forming the inner lips of
the vulva. The outer lips are the vestigial scrotum;
the inner are the vestigial raphe.

Biologically the woman occupies an intermediate
position between the man and the child.[1]

She remains related to the child in order to be
able to serve better as a mother.[2]

Various malformings of the female system may
take place, due to embryonic development suddenly
ceasing. This leads to many kinds of infantilisms in
the organic construction of the female.

The conditions of female development are negative rather than positive—that is to say . . . they depend on the absence of male hormone rather than
the presence of female hormone . . . The female
may therefore be regarded as the basic type of the
mammalian species, and the male as the more
highly differentiated type derived from it by the action of the male hormone.[3]

PHYSIOLOGY

The Male Sexual Mechanism. The simple and elementary fact behind human reproduction is that a fertile female egg awaits impregnation in the fallopian tube, and the active male sperm must find this egg and penetrate it.

The female sex apparatus is a depression to receive the sex cells; the male organs are advanced in order to expel the cells.[4]

When the male becomes sexually excited by internal stimuli, his sexual mechanism is called into play. There is a spontaneous erection of the penis, and the passageway from the testicles is thrown open. The sperm has a long way to travel through the vas deferens, through the penis, through vagina and uterus, and finally into the tiny tube where the female egg is waiting.

Nature has provided for this purpose an aggressive and active male cell. Each sperm manufactured in the complex tissues of the testes is composed of very rich and highly specialized material, and is equipped with a fine wriggling tail which gives it the power of self-locomotion.

No less than 225,000,000 cells are emitted from the man's body with each ejaculation—and every cell is a human being! *[5]

The male seminal fluid, which accompanies the sperm, has a characteristic faint odor, remarkably like that of the flowers of the Spanish chestnut.†

* The sperm itself is only ½ a human being, but such fractional qualification would ruin the esthetic veracity of the statement.

† From Van de Velde's description of semen, quoted by Parshley.[6]

When coitus and ejaculation take place, the male
sperm, millions in number and each one swimming
like a fish, begin their concentrated search for the female egg.

The instant that one of the sperm penetrates a receptive egg, the creation of a new human being has
occurred.

The male system differs markedly from that of
the female, for the male produces billions of sperm
without interruption for forty or fifty years, whereas
the girl child is born with ova already present. It
merely follows that each month one ovum is dis-
charged from an ovary.

It is of the utmost importance to make clear that
reproduction and the sex act are far more closely allied in the man's case than in the woman's, for in
the normal man the sex act is by Nature's design
specifically a reproductive act as well.[7]

A woman produces an egg usually only once a
month, and it may be viable—capable of being fertilized—for perhaps no more than twenty-four
hours. . . . Intercourse at all other times has no
reproductive significance to the female.* [8]

The Female Reproductive Function. The coordinated system of the female is merely the negative
reflection of the positive features of the male. It
functions to receive the male sperm, and to provide
shelter for the growing embryo. When the male has
sufficiently aroused the female, the organs of vulva
and vagina become flushed and congested, while

---

* If we assume, and one would not like to assume otherwise,
that the male in question is monogamous as well as normal,
intercourse at times other than when his wife is fertile will
have no reproductive significance for him either.

various glands secrete mucus in order to permit the entrance of the erect penis. This moisture is the signal that the female is ready to receive the male cells.

The female egg is incapable of self-motion. It is dependent on mechanical means for transportation from the ovary to the fallopian tube, where it is fertilized by the male sperm. It is significant that only one egg is provided each month in the female, while billions of active sperm are produced in the male for the purposes of reproduction.

If an egg is not fertilized, the currents of moisture that are always present in the female sweep it out of the body.

As an inducement to sexual union and procreation, nature has provided both men and women with sensitive pleasure-producing zones. In the male the source of pleasure is outside of his body, whereas in the female it is inside. In a fully developed woman, the strongest sexual feeling will be in the vagina. The female's vestigial penis, the clitoris, has its function in the transmission of external stimuli to the internal generative organs.

Many women say that they do not experience either pleasure or orgasm, and some have come to regard orgasm as a luxury.

And from the point of view of function, it may be said that they are right; an orgasm is for them a luxury. Whereas for the satisfactory discharge of the male function of fertilization an ejaculation, and therefore an orgasm, is indispensable, for the female function of conception an orgasm is unnecessary.[9]

Frigidity. Frigidity is a condition in females in which sexual desire or the ability to reach a climax is lacking. This is very frequent, and the theory may be advanced that the cause of this, more frequently than usually realized, is an actual organic inadequacy in the human female, perhaps resulting from the rigors of evolution. The frigidity of a wife should not interfere any more than necessary with the normal gratification of the man's sexual impulse.

Impotence. Impotence is the occasional inability of a man to obtain an erection or to carry out intercourse, either because of revulsion to the woman, indifference, or because of a psychological barrier.

We will now watch the Matriarchal biologist take over the facts of biology, producing a mirror-image of the Patriarchal account, as true and as false.

Through patriarchal eyes we observed the Tom Mix bravado of the male cell and the flower-like receptivity of the female egg. In the matriarchal account, we are not surprised to discover that the egg has become overnight the smart little administrator of fertilization, ringleader and lion-tamer, led on by destiny and a sense of right.

The male semen, on the other hand, is laboriously put together by one doubtful function after another. It begins to seem a miracle that it stays intact as long as it does, in time for the capable egg to extend a helping hand to the faltering sperm that comes so reluctantly to the bridal hour.

The matriarchal account is by no means a fair account. It is invented for the purpose of illustrating the emotional connotations of words thought by science to be objective and unprejudiced. Since the matriarchal version has not found previous expression, we will allow it a little more space and a louder grasp of adjectives.

A Matriarchal Society Writes Biology

EMBRYOLOGY

Female. The human embryo first passes through an indifferent or asexual stage in which it is not possible to distinguish female from male. In the second month, however, nature prepares for the great differentiation that is to come.

The genital projection, later the clitoris, is joined by a large genital fold, a sort of collar. This collar later becomes the outer lips of the vulva.

Along the genital projection is a cleft, a median slit which leads to the kidneys and internal genital glands. This cleft widens to form the inner lips of the vulva.

As development proceeds, the vestigial human tail, which projects from the body just as the genital tubercle does, begins to recede, taking its proper place at the base of the spine.

In like manner—but only in the female—the genital tubercle also progresses to its proper place at the head of the labia minora, or inner lips of the vulva. This interesting development of the clitoris is accompanied in the female by an extensive development of the genital fold, which becomes the pubis and outer lips of the vulva.

Thus the female human being utilizes the asexual embryonic projection (or genital tubercle) to develop the distinctive organs of clitoris and vulva.

Male. The male, we find, does not develop in any important way from the asexual or early embryonic state. His sexual organs remain in an infantile condition, displaying an early arrest of development.

Whereas in the female the genital tubercle becomes the complex and highly differentiated organ,
the clitoris, in the male the infantile genital projection remains, merely thickening and growing larger.
The penis is best described as a vestigial clitoris
which has lost much of its sensitivity.

The genital cleft, which normally remains open to
form the vulva, closes regressively in the male. During the third month nature, as though dissatisfied
with her work, rips out the stitches of the original
seam and begins again; that is to say, the glans splits
and forms a groove which closes so that the urethra
opens at the top of the penis.

The so-called raphe is the gathering line (almost
like a sewn thread) which runs longitudinally down
penis and scrotum. The raphe is the vestigial vulva,
here functionless.

Before or after birth, the male scrotum descends
outside of the body, since sperm are incapable of
tolerating the high body temperatures that the female ova find congenial. The scrotum, in which the
testes reside, is the vestigial labia majora.

Biologically the male occupies an intermediate
position between the woman and the child, or—em-
bryonically—between the fish and the human being
(for the young embryo very much resembles an am-
phibious animal).

Various malformings of the male system may take
place, due to embryonic development suddenly ceasing. This leads to many kinds of infantilisms in the
organic construction of the male.

When the sealing of the genital cleft ceases prematurely, leaving the urethral opening somewhere
between the glans and the base of the penis, an ab-

normality called *hypospadias* is produced. If the inguinal canals fail to close, a part of the intestine may find its way through in later life, causing *hernia*. Sometimes one or both testes fail to descend. The testis retained in the body is then sterile: *cryptorchidism*, a relatively common condition.*

The conditions of male development are derivative rather than positive, dependent rather than independent. This is scientifically proven by the fact that if ovaries are removed from new-born mammals, the development of the female organs is not perceptibly affected; the female retains her sexual identity.

But if we remove the testicles of young rats, we find not only the growth of all the male structures in the body arrested, but female traits soon begin to appear.[10]

It is clear that the female is the dominant human form, while the male is a more or less anomalous and accidental variation on that of the female.

PHYSIOLOGY

The Female Sexual Mechanism. The simple and elementary fact behind human reproduction is that the active female egg must obtain a male sperm before it can create new life.

The male sex apparatus is a tiny factory which continually manufactures sex cells for the female reproductive system.

When the female becomes sexually excited by

* The matriarchal biologist realizes that it is not necessary to state that the male system is more *likely* to have disorders than the female. She simply restricts her interest to the disorders of the opposite sex, communicating the impression that they are somehow more fallible.

internal stimuli, the pressure of hormones and mental images, her highly coordinated sexual mechanism is called into full play. There is a spontaneous erection of the clitoris, and a flow of blood into the fine sensitive tissues of the vagina. This causes a similar erection of this region and of the vulva, while the involuntary musculature of the vagina begins rhythmically to contract.

Secretions begin to flow which have a characteristic faint odor remarkably like that of the peach-tree blossoms of Mara, a small island off the coast of New Zealand.[11]

Because of its central importance in reproduction, the female egg has been provided with a size much greater than that of the male sperm. This contributes to its greater resistance and independence. The female egg is actually visible to the naked eye, and is the largest cell in the female body and larger than any cell in the male body. The male germ cells are unbelievably tiny, and must be magnified one hundred times in order to be visible at all.

The male sperm is produced in superfluously great numbers since the survival of any one sperm or its contact with an egg is so hazardous, and indeed improbable. The egg being more resilient, and endowed with solidity, toughness, and endurance, can be produced singly and yet effect reproduction.

In the complex tissues of the ovary one egg each month attains maturity. The ovum is composed of very rich and highly specialized material.[12] By the active pressure of its growth, its produces a slit in the wall of the ovary and escapes into the abdominal cavity. From here it works its way into the fallopian tube aided by active cilia and moisture.

The sperm are provided with a continuous enclosed passageway from the testes to the penis, thus making their conveyance as simple as possible. For the female, however, there is a remarkable gap between ovary and tube, a gap which the egg must traverse alone. When we consider that an egg never gets lost on its route, we realize the striking efficiency of the female sexual mechanism.

When the female's impulse inclines her to sexual intercourse, she must arouse the male in order to produce distension of the male organ of reproduction, the penis. This organ is composed of three sacks whose walls are riddled with blood vessels. When the male has been sufficiently stimulated, the vessels relax, thus receiving blood which causes congestion and a consequent swelling of the organ.

This response serves as a signal to the female that the male is ready for coitus. In a fully developed male, moisture will be present at the time of erection, but if this does not occur, adequate secretion is supplied by the numerous specialized glands of the female, particularly the well-known Bartholin's glands.

It is essential that the female take the initiative in the sex act, since she may have multiple orgasms and must secure contact for the clitoris. The male, on the other hand, needs only the rhythmic contractions of the vagina. If the woman obtains an orgasm before he obtains his, it is absolutely essential that she see that he too receives an orgasm. This is especially true if fertilization is desired (and the time of month propitious), but also for humanitarian reasons, in order to relieve the congestion of the penis.

At the height of the orgasm the uterus contracts

maximally, becomes erect, prolongs its neck down-
wards, and now the external os, which, owing to the
prolongation of the neck, dips into the seminal
fluid, carries out snapping movements like the
mouth of a fish. By means of these movements it
laps up the semen. . . .[13]

While the external os thus draws certain spermatozoa into the uterus, it leaves still others in the vagina. These are killed by the acids of the vagina and
then swept out of the body.

The weakened or dead sperm cells are ingested by
scavenger cells that creep out of the vaginal walls.[14]

After the sperm are drawn to the vicinity of the
egg, the egg by some little-known mechanism selects
one cell from the many present. Sometimes none of
the sperm suits the egg, in which case there is no
fertilization.

When an egg does select a male sperm, the sperm
is required to shed its wisp-like tail. Whatever temporary means the male cell had for locomotion, it is
no longer to be retained. Nature seems to be insisting that the sperm sacrifice its independence for
the larger destiny of the female egg.

For the future of the new human being now depends wholly upon the courage and acumen with
which the egg establishes its placenta and obtains
food for the active embryo.

It is clear that the sperm plays a very small and
hesitant part in this larger panorama of the creation
of life. We must not assume, however, that the
sperm is any less essential than the egg; it is a difference in function. There is no question of superiority or inferiority.

The female system differs from that of the male

in that the female egg is produced once each month with timely regularity and therefore with greater chance of being fertilized, while a margin of several million sperm is required for the fertilization of one mature egg.

Reproduction and the sex act are more closely allied in the female than in the male, because no matter how many male sperm are present, unless the female provides an ovum the sex act cannot result in fertilization. Only once each month, when the female egg is present, does intercourse have any reproductive significance for the male.[15]

The Male Reproductive Function. The coordinated system of the male is merely the negative reflection of the positive features of the female. The male functions to produce sperm to give to the female.

The sperm are manufactured by the testes and stored away. At this time they have wispy threadlike projections but are totally incapable of any motion. When the female induces a sexual response in the male, passive sperm are forced up the tubes and receive a milky secretion from the prostate. It is this secretion which gives the sperm a limited capacity for self-locomotion.

The motility of the sperm should not be exaggerated. It is the contractions of muscular tissues which force the semen from the penis. The sperm have no capacity for motion until they are supplied with the milky fluid from the prostate during ejaculation; under this influence they move jerkily about. So abortive are their movements, however, that it is no wonder millions of spare sperm are necessary.

The movement of the sperm is neither swift nor

certain. Not all sperm have effective tails, and if the prostatic secretion is deficient, there may be no movement whatever. Those sperm which do move cover about one millimetre in three minutes or one centimetre in a half hour.

The mature female egg is obliged to bide its time, not without impatience, until one of the tiny snail-like cells manages to reach it. No wonder the complicated sexual system of the female undertakes as one of its principal tasks the helpful encouragement of the dependent male cell. The fatal acids of the vagina are neutralized as much as possible by sexually stimulated glands. Active moistures supply a milieu without which the sperm would soon dry up and die.

Nature, in order to induce the male to consent to sexual union, has provided him with a sensitive pleasure-producing zone. This zone is the penis, especially the glans. The male differs from the female in that his source of pleasure is only outside the body, while the female's is both outside and inside.

Many men say that they do not experience pleasure during orgasm, and some have come to regard pleasure as a luxury.

From the point of view of function, it may be said that they are right; pleasure for men is indeed a luxury. No woman in a matriarchal society will consent to intercourse unless pleasure is involved, and therefore there can be no conception without female pleasure and satisfaction. But for the male function of supplying sperm, an emission, whether accompanied by pleasure or not, will serve to supply the egg with its needed fertilization.

Frigidity. Frigidity is a condition in males in which sexual desire or the ability to reach a climax is lacking. This is very frequent, and the theory may be advanced that the cause of this, more frequently than usually realized, is an actual organic inadequacy in the human male, perhaps resulting from the rigors of evolution. The frigidity of a husband should not interfere any more than necessary with the normal gratification of the woman's sexual impulse.

Impotence. Impotence is the occasional inability of a woman to obtain erection or to enjoy intercourse, either because of revulsion to the man, indifference, or because of a psychological barrier.

Someday, perhaps, a democratic account of the physiology of sex will be written, an account that will stress both the functional and organic aspects of reproduction. At present the functional is stressed only in connection with women: it is in them that ovaries, tubes, uterus, and vagina have endless interdependence. In the male, reproduction would seem to involve "organs" only.

Yet the sperm, just as much as the egg, is dependent on a great many related processes. There are secretions which mitigate the urine in the urethra before ejaculation, to protect the sperm. There is the reflex shutting-off of the bladder connection, the provision of prostatic secretions, and various types of muscular propulsion. The sperm is no more independent of its milieu than the egg, and yet from a wish that it were, biologists have lent their support to the notion that the human female, beginning with the egg, is congenitally more dependent than the male.

CHAPTER NINE

and then
they were one

What is it men in women do require?
The lineaments of Gratified Desire.
What is it women do in men require?
The lineaments of Gratified Desire.

WILLIAM BLAKE

When a chapter in the biology books begins, "The chief difference to be noted between the orgasm of a man and that of a woman is . . ." one is tempted to add, "is that the woman usually doesn't have one." When the tissues of the body are left sensitive and unsatisfied, physiologists describe them as "irritable." It may be more than a coincidence that women are conventionally regarded as both more sensitive and more irritable than men, and that they also less frequently have orgasm.

Many a woman protects herself against frustration by trying not to become aroused in the first place. Heroically seeking to rise above the needs of her body, she may concentrate on the birds and flowers, or attempt to regard her husband's pleasure as sufficient for both. She learns to frustrate her expectations almost before they arise, for she is aware through bitter experience that the stronger a need becomes, the more painful when frustrated.

This learned ability of the sex organs to remain neutral in the presence of normal stimuli adds to the modesty and considerateness of women, but is hardly a primitive pattern of behavior. It goes without saying that most women have learned this trick of sexual immunity long before marriage, and the husband inherits a situation he had nothing to do with originally.

Its Character

To characterize the subjective datum, orgasm, is most difficult. Those who have experienced this phenomenon sense keenly the inadequacy of any verbal equivalent; while those who have not discovered it and who seek it in a maze of kindred emotions resent the unwillingness of authors to extend the apple branch.

Questionnaires and studies concerning the occurrence of orgasm in women run into an early difficulty: women often do not know what it is they are claiming or disclaiming. If the form of the question, or the tone of the questioner, suggests that orgasm is a proper thing to have, the obedient woman answers Yes; if not, No.

Descriptions of orgasm as "great excitement" or "reaching unity" would seem to fall short of the mark. They leave out the unique element of the seizure. Sometimes the couple is said to attain Unity, or Maximum Cooperation, or Truth, Beauty and sundry other metaphysical states. While the differences between human being are nowhere more interesting and profound than in the ways they react to sex, we will attempt to isolate the peculiar attributes of this transient vision, dramatizing for the moment its unique and carnal charm.

Orgasm is best defined as that point in a continuum of sexual excitement at which an alteration of mood takes place. Granted that sexual desire is some sort of hunger, the excitement that develops around it at first increases the hunger rather than satisfying it. That is, it increases it up to the moment of orgasm. At orgasm the hunger-desire, if it does not disappear entirely, at least alters distinctly in character. While the pre-orgasmic mood is one in which the individual may feel like singing, in the orgasmic mood he is more likely to groan, and in the post-orgasmic mood to wish neither to sing nor groan, but merely to be.

Woman in this scheme is frequently the one who wants to sing and sing and sing. There is a reason for this. It is all she is allowed to do.

Orgasm differs in general from the excitement of the pre-orgasmic mood by being a temporary seizure, an agonizing species of fit which, compared with the rest of the erotic experience, is relatively crude and self-centered. In the midst of sensory excitement, orgasm with its sharp vibratory moments and high pitch of bliss catapults its owner into unsuspected chasms of desire, which create at the same instant a maximum intensity of hunger and a maximum opportunity for satisfaction. Satisfaction and hunger unite. If this comes under the head of cooperation, that is all right too.

Of all aspects of sex the climax is least understood. What happens physiologically, and how this happening differs from individual to individual, is neither fathomed nor adequately studied. Yet if the frigidity of women is seriously to be approached as a fact worthy of observation and therapy, an investigation of the phenomenon of satisfaction itself can hardly be excluded.

Orgasm involves, speaking geologically, a disturbance of the muscular and nervous system that is more staccato than the broader waves of general sensory excitement. One can postulate that sex begins with warmth and intimacy, becomes frantic and frenzied, and after orgasm or sufficient orgasms grows relaxed and vitalized. This is a rather idyllic description since the post-orgasmic mood is marked (indeed, branded) by the particular attitudes of the individuals involved: by such varieties of tenderness, revulsion, gratitude, indifference, ambivalence, and love as defy count.

If orgasm has taken place, there is a distinct alteration of mood. There is no desire to continue active intercourse; a calm settles down. The excitation of sex is over. If tension does remain, it is possibly the excitations of guilt which are set in motion by the relief of sexual tensions. As is freely suspected, humans have a hard life.

The participant in orgasm is not only restored to sanity after having been taken out of himself; he is hopelessly sober, though pleasurably so. The person who only a few moments before may have uttered ecstatic lamentations now speaks in a matter-of-fact tone, and occasionally indulges in joking remarks.

This buoyancy and humor has an unfortunate effect on that sexual partner who may not yet have reached an orgasm. She—it usually is—who still feels the humorless ravages of a Neanderthal lust.

Do women lack a sense of humor? They are less often treated to an escape from the profound—even macabre—seriousness of a pre-orgasmic mood.

No wonder sexual intercourse has through the centuries been a subject of mirth. The careless juxtaposition that nature gave to the most solemn and frantic of states and the most impersonal and calm, the orgasmic and the post-orgasmic, offers a primeval definition of wit.

An Example

A woman is horribly disillusioned by this abrupt shift in mood. The husband who only a few minutes before lavished the utmost attention upon her, praising her every virtue, begging her favor, is suddenly less concerned, almost indifferent, his arm about her shoulders somewhat limp, his tender kiss without ardor. *What!* she thinks. *Am I nothing to him now?*

We need not see this woman as a person of different constitution than he, as one who wishes flattery rather than passion, as someone with an innate desire to nag and to find fault. The fact is that she is peculiarly dependent upon her husband's initiative for her own satisfaction. At this juncture she has been greatly aroused and desires gratification. But the conclusion of her husband's orgasm leaves her with no erotic rights of her own. She has been given an opportunity and missed the boat.

That a woman does not state her disillusion as a need for sexual satisfaction is merely a concomitant of our present age. She displaces her dissatisfaction

and speaks in the only words permitted her by her
cultural milieu: she says that her husband does not
love her enough, that he is denying her *tenderness*.
This is the euphemism of the forgotten woman.

A woman is not to require passion, only tenderness, from a husband. She can scarcely mention that
she is physiologically keyed-up, unculminated, and
over-alert. She complains of more lady-like matters.
The neglected anniversary or the cigarette ashes on
the living room rug take on an amplified importance. Her biological frustration is expressing its hostility and rage through permissible female channels.

What is a typical experience in an American house-
hold? Intercourse has occurred and the husband has
reached a climax. His hopes fulfilled, he relaxes,
smiles, and murmurs to his wife (the handbooks recommend a whisper): *Are you satisfied?* The average
woman, if it is her first experience in sex, may take
this to mean: Is she happy. She responds in raptur-
ous assent. Her husband's joy at this eventuation
will seal itself in her memory: he is glad they are off
to a beautiful start.

On the other hand, if the woman has experienced
orgasm previous to marriage, her answer to his question may, on this occasion, be an abrupt *No*, swarm-
ing with ill-suppressed bitterness and anticipated
resentment. This tone of voice is perfectly commensurate with the pre-orgasmic temper. What happens next?

When the unsatisfied (and for the moment honest) woman tells her husband she is not, after all,
satisfied, it is impossible for her to ignore the slight
tightening around his brow and lips. If darkness pro-

vides the setting, the parched and hesitant silence, the reproach of a sigh, indicates that her husband is ready for the deep, restful sleep the handbooks say should follow coition.

A subordinate species such as woman has long known that the golden rule when she uses it must read: Do unto others as *they* would wish. Her sexual enjoyment was permissible as long as it enhanced his own pleasure; it is now a strange enemy of hers and his, for it wants satisfaction despite his weary desire to sleep.

With this crisis all her inhibitions and self-depreciations emerge. As a little girl her whole world was made up of people who either approved or disapproved of her. She was selfish or she was a good thoughtful girl; she pleased people or she displeased them mightily; her vocation was catering to others. The pleasure of swinging a bat or building something, or running faster than another little contemporary, was subordinate in her girl-child mores to the duty of being immediately pleasing to everyone within a certain radius.

Now having entered marriage, she knows that she is at the tender economic mercy of her husband, that it is a great privilege to be cared for just as her own father cared for her; she is especially lucky to have a man she can rely on *for her children's sake*. She also knows that it is essential for men to have sexual satisfaction, that the organs were made so that man could find such satisfaction; and has she read the handbooks, she knows that if in the natural course of his satisfying himself, she too obtains satisfaction, why then no one will reproach her and her husband

will, indeed, feel *pleased with her* for being satisfied,
that is to say, pleased that his virility has satisfied
her.

The Total Responsibility Theory

We now approach the Total Responsibility
Theory, the villain in the piece. According to this
doctrine, if the wife is satisfied it is due to the outstanding virility of the husband; while if she is not
satisfied, it is because his virility failed. What could
be more ambitious? Men have wished to appropriate the right to act in sex, and we thus find in marital relations a most unrealistic dogma: that the man
is solely responsible for the presence or absence of
sexual satisfaction in either party.

Irrespective of the inhibitions and querulities that
a woman brings to marriage, a man of proper manliness ought to be able to iron the difficulties out before she can say Jack Robinson. No wonder a husband begins to resent the recalcitrant woman; she is
a personal indictment of his manliness. No wonder
a woman begins to resent her husband since he regards her as a barometer indicating the rise and fall
of his own prestige.

While such a husband believes that sufficient virility (an occult term we shall not attempt to define)
would successfully spring the lock, the tradition of
the scapegoat is strong in human beings: he therefore suspects it is a failure in her *femininity* also,
that blocks the happy ending. We arrive at the not
unusual socio-human situation in which only one
person is Responsible but everybody is Blamed.

Returning to the wife of our example, she had

just admitted that she was not satisfied. It is unusual if the husband has a second erection and intercourse is repeated; and it is possible, or probable, that his wife will still whisper No to his inquiry. Women's lack of orgasm is a persistent thing. Enter the sex booklets. While tension is increasing at this point, we will assume that the husband knows the handbooks backwards and forwards. He has tried method A of *You Too Can Find Marriage Harmony*; he realizes he must now resort to method B. With method B, that of manual friction, orgasm is achieved.

The humane husband waits until she has reached this happiness before projecting an account of his disappointment and gentle reproof. But sooner or later in the literate circles of which we write, the husband informs her that method B is vaguely contraband, and will she please try to adjust to method A which he likes ever so much better? She promises.

Men customarily regard any such statistics as 80 per cent non-orgasm in women as comprising all-wives-other-than-mine. Let us not be premature. A woman can suppress external indications of an orgasm even when she has one, which makes it harder to tell when she does not. While involuntary contractions of the vagina may take place during orgasm, these are in most women weak. Strong muscular contractions can be made voluntarily, not necessarily with accompanying emotion. They are as voluntary as clenching the fist. The woman's verbal testimony is, therefore, all that can be accepted as proof of orgasm, and the word of an intimidated woman is not always to be relied on.

A woman whose chief education as a child was in

pleasing others will feel completely stifled by her
husband's disappointment, either at her not ob-
taining an orgasm at the moment he does, or ob-
taining none at all. It is a rare and resilient female
who persists in shaking her head in reply to a
husband's anxious whisper: Are you satisfied?

Sooner or later, chances are she will try something
different: she will murmur *Yes.* Then what rewards,
what adulation, what happiness flows in a sweet
breathlessness toward her! She sees her beloved's
brow relax, the deep restful sleep come on. She
knows herself to be an unnatural woman but no
one else need know it. And that is always half the
battle with someone whose training has been to
please and to be approved. Only later, and
unnoticeably, does she begin to resent intercourse
and her husband's enjoyment and her own lies. For
presently he no longer asks if she is satisfied; it has
happened so often that it will always happen, and if
it doesn't (impossible thought) she will then let
him know.

It is hard to feel sad about these misled husbands.
For if they had not betrayed in so many ways their
anxiety, their tenseness, their disappointment when
their wives "failed" them, they might never have
been lied to at all. What then? Shall women acquire
peace through distraction, spin wool, weave gar-
ments, and return to their ancient occupations at
the hearth?

There Must Be a Way

As accredited cartographers of the sex impulse,
the authors of marital handbooks have made up

their minds way in advance as to what is right and proper in love. If sexual satisfaction has not occurred after following their simple directives for the perfect sex act, the booklets exchange glances with one another and admit grudgingly of alternative approaches. While most books are in favor of an orgasm for women, they cannot quite suppress their disapproval of methods secondary, tertiary, or dromedary. The most widely recommended of these secondary methods is the friction orgasm. Opponents of this method claim that women become addicted to it and cease reaching for the ideal.

The danger of omitting orgasm in any single instance is twofold. The sexual experience quickly becomes associated with frustration, and this brings with it a raft of conflicts and inhibitions, especially if the woman feels her normality is on trial. In many a marriage sex has become an arena in which the man's virility and the woman's normality are both on trial—often in the role of contesting gladiators.

Another result of omitting orgasm in cases where it does not occur during intercourse is that the woman may take it upon herself to induce one privately. There is no adequate study of this, but it is significant that results of a questionnaire by Dr. Katherine B. Davis reveal that of married women who mentioned autoerotic experience, one-fourth had continued after marriage.[1] In seeking to conform to the Total Responsibility Theory, women may sometimes feel they are left with no alternative.

While the power and resourcefulness of the human male is vast and inexhaustible, one wonders if he should volunteer to arouse, by sheer prowess, any given maiden of twenty-odd years. The Sleep-

ing Beauty really was asleep all those years, but the
modern girl is only pretending to be asleep. She is
actually undergoing, through childhood and youth,
a course in frigidity that has become basic training
for all well-bred, maladjusted American females.

CHAPTER TEN

the good will hour

*Love between man and woman is really just
a kind of breathing.*

D. H. LAWRENCE

Radio's Good Will Hour illustrates America's general attitude toward marital difficulties: *Remember, Madam, YOU married him!* is its reply. Everything depends on making a difficult decision and sticking to it; in this respect Mr. Anthony and Denis de Rougemont agree to the last man. If it happens to be a decision of the past, this only makes it more a trial of combat. Anything can be made to work if you just want it to enough. We are a nation of boosters, and the Rotarian spirit pervades marriage as well as real estate.

In high clear tones a sex booklet will instruct the husband in sure-fire methods of bringing joy to his wife. Stress is less on resourcefulness than on dogged adherence to the rules. There is the correct overture, the correct sensation, the correct setting, the correct lapse of time, the correct satisfaction and the incorrect satisfaction, the correct preliminary and the correct aftermath. Marriage has become a game of chess in which checkmate is the rule, but you've got to frustrate the other person according to Hoyle or you don't get the loving cup inscribed with NON-DEVIANT.

The perfect marriage is like the gold the ancient alchemists were hotly in pursuit of. It didn't matter how often the chemical constituents failed them: something must have been wrong with the recipe. Thus perfect compatibility in marriage is said to be simple, but you or you or the clock on the wall is interfering with the production of gold. Marriage takes two; it requires adults ready for self-discipline. Chronic infelicity should not promote separation, writes Mary Baker Eddy, for "if one is better than the other, as must always be the case, the other pre-eminently needs good company."

Whatever Became of the Perfect Sex Act?

A person scouring books for advice on love is struck at once by the patience required of everyone. The husband is to be patient with his wife and the wife is to be patient with her husband. Yet patience may not be the best therapy at all. To combine passion with a calm concern or grave forbearance is like trying to run a race and work out geometric theorems at the same time. This may suit some temperaments but not others. It depends whether (in Kierkegaard's terms) you are trying to pass from the esthetic phase into the ethical.

Marriage may need a theatrical element most of all. Babbittry, which is virtually a doctrine of satiation, received a setback recently when science discovered that the superior intelligence of young rats to older rats came about merely because the young rats were hungrier. If the older rats received shorter rations of food, they demonstrated just as much cleverness and sensibility as the young in traversing mazes and solving the problems of the laboratory. Similarly, the presumed "masochism" of the poet or esthete has its calculated result in a practical and demonstrable accentuation of sensitivity and reflectiveness.

In the famous case of multiple personality, when *Doris* became the child-personality *Margaret*—one of her many metamorphoses—she could hear a watch ticking thirty-one feet away, normal hearing range being only five feet. If spontaneity can sharpen perceptions this much, perhaps we should try it more.

Too much comfort may be a handicap. Walter B. Cannon's demonstration of the acceleration of the sympathetic nervous system under the stimulus of pain and emotion is relevant here; satiation destroys drive.[1] Comfort, however, is what pervades descriptions of the perfect setting as outlined in books on sex. They warn that everything be in readiness long before the event; caution and foresight are the maxims. It must not be too early in the morning or too late at night, too soon in the fall or too late in the spring.

Yet surely the mating of humans is not as precarious as that of the wood frog, in whom sexual excitement reaches its peak at 52° F. and is almost wholly wanting at 45° F.

Frequency and position usually fall under one dogmatic prescription or another. Yet as Dr. Dickinson writes, "Frequency gives no clue to vigor, interest or erotic satisfaction. Once a week may be more completely satisfactory than daily or oftener." [2] Concerning the usual position assumed during inter-

course, it is reversed in the earliest Stone Age
drawings, as well as in the murals of Pompeii.[3] In
both these cases the woman is uppermost.

Romance, Passion, and Companionship

A movie blurb that attempts to satisfy the general love-cravings of mankind reads something like
this one:

E As constant as the stars . . . as en-
V chanting as a dream . . . lifting you to
O the supreme heights of exquisite rapture . . .
L as it seeks fulfillment.

As constant as the stars has the sober accent of
companionship, a binding association. *As enchant-
ing as a dream* lends the charm and the inno-
cence of early romance. *Lifting you to the supreme
heights of exquisite rapture*: it is typical of the movies that passion is the last thing on the agenda.

Paradoxically, the sex booklets, though infused
with sweetness and light and guarded over by the
golden rule, nevertheless orient themselves around
passion as the important factor in marital relations.
Maybe this is because passion so closely precedes
the post-orgasmic mood of calmness, absence of
sexual drive, return of rationality, and other attributes of the law-abiding citizen. While the books,
the modern ones, set out to persuade us that sex
isn't bad and that passion is good, one finds them
reaching with relief the moment in which the lover
(or patient) can be advised to "drop into a deep
restful sleep." They seem, in other words, to be

exalting passion with the intention of getting it over with as quickly as possible.

European writers on sex approach their subject with more candor and enthusiasm than most of us dare to in the New World. Dr. Kahn, for example, has a gayety of style very different from most American tracts. "A cry, a tear, a sigh filled with pain and pleasure, followed by a smile, and from among the parting clouds of the marital heaven Hymen, the god of the nuptial night, smiles triumphantly." Compare with this an American writer reaching imaginative heights: "The giving of gifts, the saying of 'sweet nothings' sitting close to each other, holding hands and hugging and kissing are all manifestations of this fundamental characteristic of personal affection." [4]

Only Dr. Robert Latou Dickinson has consistently combined dignity, accuracy, and wit concerning what he has called "the pervicacious gonad úrge in human beings." Not only as an eminent gynecologist and a relentless scientist, but in the humor and élan that invests his superb literary style, he is by all odds the Titan in this field.[5]

To return to our discussion of romance, passion, and companionship, one of the common complaints in marriage is that one party to the cause prefers one aspect of love to the others. The prosecuting party generally produces an elaborate argument to prove that one of these is more normal and more important. Romance-advocates claim that passion burns itself out, and that companionship lacks warmth. To their physician these philosophers exclaim that *he* always wants one thing, and never has time for affection.

Those who believe the satisfaction of passion to
be the central aim in love are not so foolish in a
sexually nervous culture as to base their thesis on a
selfish ejaculation phase. They dignify their viewpoint by saying that the rest of the sex act is all right
in its place, but its role is purely preliminary. The
male instinct is to drive irresistibly ahead to physical
gratification. This argument, as logical and as prej-
udiced as its predecessor, regards affection as inferior to passion because the former precedes the latter.
It is physiologically true that romantic love, as a
longing, tends toward fulfillment, but life tends
toward decay, and spring toward fall. Shall we
subscribe to these end-products as superior to their
antecedents?

Those who choose companionship as the be-all
and often the end-all of marital love regard both
passion and romance as preliminary to the equanim-
ity of satisfied longing, comradely friendship, and
social usefulness. They argue that passion and romance are childish and passing phases; the adult
form of love is a state of hardihood and reason.
With romance, they warn, one is likely to get *hurt*.

These discrete departments of love clearly relate
to the physiological states of pre-orgasmic, orgasmic, and post-orgasmic. That the sex act should
have been dramatized around the ejaculation phase,
at least for one half the population, is merely the
bias of the century. By seeing sex as a dynamic combination of many types of experience, each justifi-
able and unique and related to physiological sources,
a woman need not feel unnatural because her desire for "romance" survives his. There is no biolog-

ical reason why *his* orgasm should have gratified *her*.

Fortunately, in marital disagreements while it is easy to obtain a quorum it is impossible to obtain a majority vote that is not also unanimity.

The Perfectly Happy Couple

When the anti-trust law is invoked against the monopoly of a patent, the defense counsel—according to Thurman Arnold—is likely to conjure up a popular symbol of the Penniless Inventor. Not a product of elaborate industrial laboratories or high-salaried groups of men, the patented article or process is thought to be the creation of some lonely and rugged individualist, whose humble livelihood depends on a certain clause of the patent law. If investigation is made of a railroad, the corporation investors assume the pale faces of widows and orphans overnight.

So it is in the field of sex. If one asks whether certain legal and social regulations contribute to the happiness of the people involved, all minds converge involuntarily to the defense of the perfect couple, that healthy, happy, high-spirited trio, father, mother and child, whose prototype, one would think, inhabited every home in the nation.

A perfectly happy couple was once seen. It was in the Pennsylvania Station during the war. Most of the trains were hours late, and hundreds of us loitered about, sitting on our worn suitcases and feeling disreputable and morose. Suddenly a most refreshing sight appeared in the midst of the crowd. A tripod was set up, camera and heavy black cloth.

Before it stood a soldier, his young wife and their
child, talking to an MP. They were waiting for the
cameraman to be ready.

Everyone within a certain radius turned toward
them with wonder and a sense of revelation. The
young woman was charming, well dressed, benev-
olent and unspoiled. Her hair was lustrous and a
natural golden brown. The curls were brushed up
into crest-tipped waves with the back curls loose and
short. On her head was a velveteen skullcap with a
chaplet of sable muskrat. She was smiling with that
curious embarrassed intimacy a young wife has
when under the public gaze.

The young man seemed even more shy than she,
though he stood straight and boyish, tall and attractive, at her side. His expression was grave, as though
timid before his child's charm and his wife's beauty.
Where were they going? Possibly on a furlough, a
vacation. They were celebrities of some sort, or the
children of celebrities, for the cameraman was
assiduously adjusting his lens.

A curious mixture of expressions appeared on
the faces of the crowd. The men seemed on the
whole very interested, curious, and considerably
happy about the pretty girl. But the women—
did one imagine it?—wore a bitter and envious
look. America makes such stringent demands on
its women. We are expected to be ravishingly beautiful, to have perfect children, a humble adoring
husband; and to look rested and youthful in the
midst of all these attainments.

That was the charming thing about this family
group. The little girl, about six, was bright and
merry and seemed on her good behavior. She had

blond curls and piquant features. Underneath her
spice-colored coat was a little linen dress, water-
melon pink, with fringed sailor collar. She wore a
perky Dutch bonnet and carried a clean rag doll
whose checked apron and toothy grin were a delight
to behold.

No wonder the crowd gaped. It is one thing to
have a child well dressed and well behaved, and
another to remain—as mother—so cool and well
groomed oneself. The young wife straightened the
hat of the little girl, which did not need straighten-
ing, and patted her shoulder affectionately. She was
laughing at something her husband had said to the
MP.

Finally the camera was ready. The cameraman's
assistants posed the young family, commandeering
a baggage van full of rich ox-hide luggage, hat boxes,
extra tweed coats, golf clubs in burnished calf hold-
ers. We might well sigh at it all. The father was asked
to hold the little girl in his arms, which he did with
alacrity. The wife stood young and excitedly at his
side, looking up at him. Her blue cardigan jacket
was crisp; over her arm was a topcoat of coral wool.
The child stretched out its arm and jingled a brace-
let of brightly colored glass animals. And then with
the special little look that children reserve for
their fathers, she turned and looked down at the
soldier, who grinned back at her like a boy. Here
indeed was the perfect couple, everything new, still
exciting.

Suddenly the camera clicked, and the picture
was taken. The setting and the characters began to
disintegrate. A porter hurried up and removed the
baggage van. One of the cameraman's assistants

came forward and handed the young woman a cardboard hat box. She moved a short distance away and changed her shoes hastily. The young soldier pulled an MP band from his pocket and laboriously worked it over his shirtsleeve. The MP to whom he had been talking handed him a gun in a holster.

The girl with the hat box, nodding politely to the two men, disappeared into the crowd without so much as a backward glance. By now the camera and tripod had been packed away, and a tall brunette woman, haggard and gaunt, came forward and took the little china-doll girl by the hand, scolding her for something. The soldier walked off, blushing, with his comrade. The little girl was smiling, but her mother was irritated about something and gesticulated angrily to the cameraman.

We in the crowd felt sad and dejected. The unattainable bubble had escaped again. The next chance we would have to see this charming scene might well be on the next cover of *Good Housekeeping*. Where else?

Was it W. H. Auden who called attention to the strange fact that there are so many happy marriages and so many unhappy people?

CHAPTER ELEVEN

a new generation

Abstinence sows sand all over
The ruddy limbs and flaming hair
WILLIAM BLAKE

Two Forces stand over the child, influencing, enforcing, encouraging, dissuading it at every step. These forces are the Angel and the Adder of childhood, Reward and Recrimination, the one floating down with sugared gifts, praises or merely promises, and the other descending with fire and brimstone, social ostracism and the birch rod. Mother is generally the prime mover behind these, but there are also fathers, uncles, aunts, brothers and sisters, as well as the child's own needs and preferences.

A mother may scold while an older brother rewards—and for the same behavior. All these facts enter into the child's experience, ambivalent, confused, contradictory as they may be, and when they have come to terms with the child's own needs, he begins to adopt preferences and develop character. The patterns of the past influence his later actions, his anticipation of reward and punishment and the hierarchy of his needs. For if a very small and unimportant desire meets with an avalanche of recrimination, the child may dismiss it as too troublesome. Or he may repress a strong insistent need because it arouses terror in him merely to contemplate it, so deeply has it become associated with punishment.

What a mother believes is a very moderate admonition may fall on a child with tremendous and staggering weight. She is free to judge his need, and therefore his deed, as insignificant, but the child may think otherwise. In matters of sex, mothers consistently underestimate the importance, and therefore the effect, of their disciplinary measures. A mother can deliver a momentous punishment to her child, and then with the cooperation of her own inhibitions, repress the importance of what she has just done, both for herself and the child.

The force of any punishment lies in part in the consistency with which it is repeatedly enforced. Whether a mother shouts discipline at her child or whispers it does not at face value indicate the consistency with which the commands are enforced. Mothers who shout unrestrainedly at their active male children often turn out to have at home a large brood of quiet, obedient daughters. In fact, shouting frequently accompanies lack of enforcement. The quiet-spoken mother who administers nothing but polite requests in the form of rhetorical questions may nonetheless have in her tone a positiveness and finality that insures obedience.

This note of positiveness especially permeates injunctions about sex. No exceptions are tolerated, and for the most part the mother's voice adopts a strong tone of alienation of affection which strikes particular horror into a child of two or three. It does not matter whether the child understands the words that are uttered or not.

Mothers prefer to think their sex teaching is

"neutral" toward children of two years. This is because they do not like to think any sex need is present at all. However, if sex behavior, as in touching or curiosity, is unimportant or absent in children, how do mothers explain their own severity in regard to these manifested activities? For some reason sex behavior receives the most stringent taboo of all, excretory behavior at the wrong time or place receives the next most stringent punishment, and disobedience in food habits—eating with fingers, spilling, and so on—is most often tolerated. These three forms of disobedience are clearly arranged in the order of their embarrassment to the mother, and not with regard to the needs of the child.

In the developing of sex attitudes, invisible forms of Recrimination are especially decisive. Tone of voice is a major weapon, with social pressure its suffocating concomitant. The mother speaks softly but in her very decisiveness the child feels a Wall of Disapproval moving slowly toward it, giving the full effect of solitary confinement.

Nor should we ignore the invisible Rewards. When a child takes a piece of candy, the flavor of the candy and the adventure of the enterprise will be weighed against the punishment received, if any. In sex behavior the punishments which touching-in-public receive are weighed against the rewards that self-exploration-in-private earns. If sex taboos held off for a few years in the child's experience, this conscious weighing of the pros and cons of sexual enjoyment would be a leading factor in the adult adjustment. As it is, superstition early takes hold, and nameless forgotten fears preside, especially in the sex training of girls.

The conditioning processes of the first two years
are of overwhelming significance. Rewards and recriminations are handed out daily, whether by
tone of voice or facial expression or verbal command.
And in these earliest years a *differential* training
begins for boys and girls concerning two of their
basic needs, the urinary and the sexual. What is
meant by "sexual" in this instance is simply that
nerve endings do exist, touching produces pleasure; and pleasure is in one sex rewarded and in the
other punished.

Pleasure and Proscription

One of the basic needs is urination, a type of behavior whose goal is relief and whose performance
early receives the concentrated attention of the
mother. In disciplining and guiding the satisfaction
of this need, a mother brings to the task her two
able-bodied helpers, reward and recrimination.
Good habits receive her love and sworn devotion
while bad habits find her love withdrawn and punishment delivered.

Having no idea what a profound influence it would
have on the frigidity of women, nature instituted a
marked difference in the urinary provisions of
male and female. The male has a visible, mani-
fest organ for urination. Further, this organ is not
only the urinary channel but the sexual-reproduc-
tory as well; it is likewise the region of most intense
pleasure sensations.

In the female the urinary is one channel (the
urethra), the reproductory-sexual is another (the
vagina), and a primary pleasure zone (the clitoris)

is distinct from both of these. In urination, no "organ" appears to be involved. This is truly a biological difference between male and female, but what happens next is an arbitrary program of social conditioning that favors the male.

To train a child in good urinary habits, usually during the second year, the stress is upon modesty and cleanliness. In enforcing the rule of cleanliness, the mother encourages appropriate handling techniques in the boy. The girl, however, is issued a strict hands-off policy.

Thus in response to a basic and elemental need, the urinary function, the mother praises the boy for touching the penis and handling it efficiently. Since the penis also happens to be the erogenous center, his touching elicits pleasure, however diffuse. At the moment of pleasure, the boy is praised. Of course, the mother intends to praise him for correct urination only, but for a child (or an adult) praise becomes diffused over the entire context of the experience. The praise for proper urination diffuses over the situation as a whole, including the central performer in this instance, the penis. Without the participation of the penis, there can be no proper urinary habits, no praiseworthy performance, and no rewards from Mother.

In the little girl, only one thing is punished: touching. Touching interferes with cleanliness; touching is unnecessary. Praise for the girl depends on a sternly impersonal attitude toward the whole thing. Curiosity and handling are all right for boys, but it is not appropriate for her. Thus at any given moment of pleasure, of contact with sensory zones, the girl is promptly punished. This punishment is very stringent and consistently enforced. It is administered with disgust by the mother and received with shame by the child.

At the moment of sensory pleasure, the boy is praised. At the moment of pleasure, the girl is punished. Here is a differential training of the sexes which is the first step in frigidity: the inhibition of sexual pleasure due to shame or guilt.

Suppose the penis were simply a urinary channel, without erogenous qualities, and suppose the male's sexual organ, equivalent to the glans and analogous to the clitoris, were small, separate, and somewhat hidden. The mother would consistently praise the son for adequate handling of the penis during urination; she would punish him for any touching of the pleasure zone. He would therefore develop severe inhibitions in regard to sexual pleasure, and feel pride and happiness in regard to the penis.

Suppose in the female the sexual organ, the clitoris, were also the urinary organ. The performance of this organ would then receive the praise of the mother, and the praise would seem to include any erogenous pleasures included in the context of the act. The child would develop much pride and confidence in regard to this organ and its potentialities.

As it is, the female possesses the same sensory erogenous nerves as the male, but is not allowed to experience them. She is specifically forbidden to. There is no "reason" for her to elicit such pleasure responses. But several times a day the boy finds excellent and approved reasons for extending his acquaintance with his own region.

After a week, a month, or a year of these excur-

sions, it is no wonder that the little boy begins to
regard his sexuo-urinary organ as a distinct asset.
When he learns to talk, we can be sure that one of
his first offices will be to inform his little sister of
his remarkable possession. Then comes the discovery: *None for you? How jolly sad!* If he demonstrates
what a beautiful parabola this organ is capable of
creating, the little girl is further impressed. This
parabola undoubtedly offers a primitive and unique
esthetic appeal which the girl cannot compete with.

Confronted with her brother's possession, the
little girl examines her own situation. While the
male clearly regards his own organ as friendly,
rewarding, and eminently approachable, her own
body offers nothing of a like nature. Indeed, in
her case is there any organ involved at all? Praise for
her was always for being quiet, modest and non-
curious: that is, for *not* doing things that brought
pleasure.

The Search for the Grail

Little philosophers that they are, children seek to
reinforce the rewards they meet up with in life and
mitigate the punishments. In colloquy with other
youngsters they tend to live over the rewards they
enjoyed at home while seeking to undermine the
parental recriminations. For the little boy entering school, his sexuality has for him two aspects, one
good and one bad. The penis has been steadily
approved for its urinary function, including the
socially-approved handling. It has also been punished
—for any handling that did not relate to the urinary
office. His organ has a half-and-half virtue about it.

Added to the merit side are the pleasures it may
have afforded him privately. The little boy arrives
at age six with a measure of confidence and pride
in himself.

We do not mean to underestimate the negative
conditioning he has probably received. Since all
punishment must be judged in terms of intensity
and consistency, the praise he received for good
urinary practices may have been casual; while the
punishment for self-exploration may have been
severe. In this case he will have something less than
a half-and-half approval of himself.

However, where a boy emerges with a fifty-fifty
confidence, his sister is likely to emerge with an
eighty-twenty lack of confidence. In discussions with
his friends, the boy promptly seeks to build up the
approval factors and depreciate the ignominy factors.
They are happy to aid him in this, because it automatically increases their own ratio of self-approval.
Older boys contribute immeasurably to the ideolog-
ical process, and after five or ten years the penis
has gained greatly in prestige.

Alas, the boy's little sister finds no such freedom
of speech operating among her female chums. Girls
enter first grade only after having completed a six-
year course in the condemnation of this region. The
twenty percent approval we have allowed was in all
probability acquired privately, under the most
furtive conditions. This Shangri-La, while known
to all of them, is not a subject about which nice
girls speak.

How often the girl ventures on the subject of sex
for the first time with a boy rather than a girl would
be interesting to know. Whether it is a boy she con-

sults or a girl, however, she will find it practically impossible to reduce her sense of ignominy by more than ten or twenty percent. Talking it over with little boys, she is told what she doesn't have. It is an absolute fact: she lacks the one thing the boy respects most. While her own region turns out to be of considerable curiosity to the opposite sex, it lacks their dash and bravado. Nor does the little girl even pretend to find the fun in it that the boy finds in his.

In seeking the grail of Public Approval, one would think that other little girls, in search of approval, would join forces. But they feel the same overwhelming sense of inferiority she does. The prestige of the penis appears to be universal. The girl is confronted with nothing but facts. She might make a scientific canvass of all boys and girls of her age, trying to find out if *any* girl exists who thinks she is made as admirably as a boy, or if *any* boy would like to trade constitutions with a girl. Her survey could not be more empirical, nor the result more devastating. With a precision impossible in almost any other scientific field, the little girl finds a one-hundred percent admission by both sexes that to have a penis is preferable to not having one.

Perhaps our little girl at this moment begins actively to experience a flourish of jealousy. If her state of mind is to be termed penis envy, it must be added that it is based less on her knowledge of the opposite sex than on ignorance of her own, an ignorance shared by many medical men, most psychoanalysts, and certainly by Freud himself.[1]

By the time a boy reaches the age of ten, he has

acquired the additional knowledge that girls are physically weaker, require more protection, cannot stay out as late, and are often denied the games he finds so life-giving. The basis on which she is denied these privileges is girldom, or a difference in bodily structure.

At this age the "difference between the sexes" is not that girls have babies and boys do not, but that boys have an organ and girls have none. If the girl felt the taboo on her organism would be removed later by the socially approved function of childbearing, she might not suffer quite the same sense of inadequacy. But society, fearing she will embark on the approved mission before the approved time, furnishes her with very little information on this score.

By fifteen, a boy begins to anticipate his future role as breadwinner and protector. While this prospect may not appeal to him particularly, it is infinitely preferable to being a girl, the very thought of which repels him. Cooking and housecleaning, or wearing dresses, inspire the deepest disgust. Interestingly enough, a good many girls at fifteen have not made up their mind whether or not they agree with him. Whatever girls think at fifteen, at eighteen they know it is no longer permissible, that is, socially rewarding, to weigh aloud the pros and cons of being a girl. And after all, only girls can have babies. From this time on, the girl adopts those goals for which society promises to reward her.

Suppose a girl goes on to college. Everything she learns in this institution of higher learning reinforces, point by point, what her little brother lisped to her at the age of four. Fact: that the female equipment is decidedly inferior from a sexual viewpoint, though not from a reproductory one. As pleasure organs, the female has infantile vestiges, and penis envy is based on the realistic fact that girls lack an organ of adequate sexual potentiality. If the clitoris remains sensitive it means that the girl is "sexually anesthetic," a most peculiar situation semantically.

When these college-trained women marry, they make rapid acquaintance with the Total Responsibility Theory. Again they learn that everything their little brother told them that day was true. They hear all over again who has prior rights and whose needs are most important for the species. Why? The possession of one set of organs rather than another—facts, nothing but facts.

Every Child an Admirable Byrd

"Men have died from time to time and worms have eaten them, but not for love."
ROSALIND, in As You Like It

People do not die from excess of love or the want thereof. Most mothers understand thoroughly this bit from the Bard, if only from their own experience, and it has left them with a remarkably free hand concerning sex instruction of the young. While neighbors and relatives hover about, checking on food habits and cleanliness, worrying about the child's survival and insisting that mother's charge exhibit rosy cheeks and a healthy appetite, the gentle and refined measures that are daily taken to massacre sexuality in children go unnoticed.

Since the self-exploratory tendency in children
places this impulse among the corps of basic needs,
it is disturbing to find with what unceasing
punishment it is checked. Indeed if children did
not retire now and again to elicit mildly rewarding
responses from forbidden zones, they might actually
take their mothers seriously, and resolve never to
go near the dreaded site again—a matter that would
eventually have to be taken up with the Depart-
ment of Forestry. Wise in the extreme, ever count-
ering the punishment inflicted by parents, the primitive nerve centers continue to offer their own
rewards.

When questioned, parents will admit they are
prepared to see sexuality emerge somewhat before
the child's first ballot is cast. But how many are
prepared for further facts? The women who answered Dr. Davis' questionnaire stated the age at
which autoerotic interests began as anywhere from
five years to eight, and on. Some women recalled
interest beginning at the age of six, or at seven;
while a marked number initiated the practice at
eight. By the age of sixteen, nearly sixty percent
of the women who practiced autoeroticism at one
time or another had discovered this practice. Some
of them stopped within a year, half carried on from
ten to twenty years, and a few for thirty.[2]

It may be asked why, considering these facts, anyone should worry about the suppression of the sex
impulse. Women seem to have discovered a great
many things for themselves, and parental strictures
did not wholly deter them from exercising their
knowledge. However, is it possible that the word

autoeroticism, or masturbation, is interpreted differently by the two sexes?

The majority of males place the time at which autoeroticism began between the age of twelve and seventeen, while the practice in women is said to begin for the most part between the age of five and eleven. The mode or peak of beginnings for women is at the eighth year. Now, the men are citing an age at which orgasm is usually discovered, but women are in many cases citing an age long before puberty, when orgasm is for the most part impossible.

While the majority of women (60 percent) said autoerotic practices began *before* the age of seventeen, the majority (62 percent) of those women who had experienced orgasm said that it was discovered *after* the seventeenth year. There is evidence, therefore, that the definition of autoeroticism for women does not include orgasm as a necessary element. Boys said to discover autoeroticism for the most part between the ages of twelve and seventeen, have probably simultaneously linked discovery of orgasm with this word. We can hardly assume that no handling, no sensory pleasure, no exploration takes place in males before the age of twelve. Rather is the definition of the word autoeroticism reserved for those sensory pleasures which culminate in orgasm and ejaculation.

Women in citing the beginning of autoeroticism anywhere from age five on, might appear to be reaching sexual maturity sooner than men. Instead they probably have defined autoeroticism (and applied its moral stigma) to any minor investigations at all. Males tend to dismiss the juvenile tactual pleasures that precede puberty as mere child's play, while females are convinced that they indulged in every known or imagined sin when—at the age of five—they touched themselves gingerly.

If women do not find orgasm involved in auto-eroticism, it helps explain why they do not expect orgasm from marriage. While girls, as boys, begin investigation of their sensory centers extremely early in life, girls bring to this experimentation relatively more modesty, uncertainty, and inhibition. Ironically enough, this may be why they cite an earlier age for the commencement of autosexual practices. Fewer women move at puberty into a more adult experience of sex.

Logic as the Lapdog of the Status Quo

The magic of Either/Or helps us overlook embarrassing injustices. With kindergarten logic we try to reduce everything to the rain-pattering formula: "Either it is raining, or it is not raining." No wonder Keats feared the destruction of the rainbow: *is* it raining or *isn't* it?

On the scales at the grocery, thanks to the energies of science, the vague realm betwixt one pound and two is marked with minute degrees which possess definite names, ounces. We are not satisfied to know that a bag of potatoes either weighs two pounds or does not weigh two pounds. We want to know exactly what fraction of a pound is involved, since each fraction affects our purse.

But when we come to a consideration of marriage,

love, and sexual delight, we do not treat these with as much respect as merchandise. "Well," we say, "either a woman experiences pleasure or she does not experience pleasure." We do not demand names for those minute and complex degrees between pleasure and non-pleasure. Surely the language could provide some thought on this subject, if society provided some interest.

We scrupulously examine the lines sketched on the scale of weights, while toward the non-negotiable degrees of pleasure—especially in women—we turn a deaf eye, pleading for an abandonment of the nuisance of science and a return to the syllogisms of our fathers. "If sex implies pleasure, and pleasure implies satisfaction, then all sex must imply satisfaction."

But we cannot rely on a form that reads: Either sexual interest (being rewarded) will continue, or (being punished) it will not continue. A sexual need, persistently checked by guilt, may continue in an overt way, but with such painful reservations, repercussions, gnawings, and rancid shame that its spirit is indistinguishable from pabulum.

Outwardly the Either/Or principle may seem to hold. Marriage is entered upon, homes are furnished, dinner parties given, children are brought into the world, insurance policies taken out, and the individual dies with a devoted family gathered at the bedside. But the petty frustrations in spite of which the happy marriage was effected—these go to the grave with the bearer.

The Incisive Approach

As a rest from the repressions of modernity, our Bauhaus era of functional furniture and functional frigidity, we might turn momentarily to a time not so long ago when the taboo on sexuality was neither so invisible nor psychological as it is today. In the America of the late 1800s, leading medical journals carried articles with titles such as these: *Surgical Treatment of Hopeless Cases of Masturbation and Nocturnal Emissions; History of a Case of Death from Onanism; Removing the Clitoris in Cases of Masturbation Accompanied with Threatening Insanity; Opium as a Tonic and Alternative.* Today medical journals seldom mention these topics, either because such phenomena are no longer feared, or possibly because they cannot be said to lead to sterility, melancholia, and death, as was then supposed.

In 1867 the London Obstetrical Society expelled one of its members, Dr. Baker Brown (as the *Journal of the American Medical Association* put it) "because he amputated the clitoris so very frequently." [3] Dr. Brown believed he had found a cure for certain forms of hysteria, insanity, and epilepsy in women. When expelled from the Society he asserted that he was being persecuted merely for being in the vanguard of medical science.

At the annual meeting of the Gynecological Society of Boston, January 13, 1887, a physician reported a case of *Melancholia, Masturbation; Cured by Removal of Both Ovaries.* [4] To read this report is to appreciate the revolutionary humanity that

Freud introduced into the world. The patient, a woman of thirty-three, had complained of pain in both ovaries and a temptation toward autoeroticism; she "begged that some operation might be performed in hope of relief." The physician consequently removed her ovaries, an operation which in those days was quite dangerous although (as he added reassuringly) "not as dangerous as a major amputation."

A month later the Society met again, to learn whether the experiment had had its effect. "Clitoridectomy is inefficient, but removal of the ovaries has in some cases been done with advantage." It was too soon to know whether the improvement was permanent, but the surgeon stated that his patient was now "entirely free from melancholia and sexual passion"; she had described her improved mental condition by saying "a window has been opened in heaven."

A physician who had been called in for consultation took the floor to say that "of all triumphs of surgery none equal this operation." Formerly the patient had been "miserable," he said, but she was now "quiet and pleasant"—two adjectives which might be thought to cover all attributes suitable to a woman. The speaker recommended that the treatment be taken into asylums where many cases, he felt, would benefit.

A number of physicians present regarded the cure as primarily "moral"—that is, psychological. One suggested that "Americans are given to overdoing things," and were likely to fall into this error in surgery also. The cruelest comment came from a woman physician present who said the patient was "not now more mutilated than before" and "children springing from such parentage are not wanted."

Of two "nymphomania" cases reported in the *American Journal of Obstetrics* [5] in 1907, one turns out to be a child of eight, the other a married woman who had admitted to strong sexual desire despite the complete absence of vagina, uterus, tubes, and ovaries—an omission on Nature's part. The sensitivity of the clitoris was enough to label her "nymphomanic."

Under "Transactions of the American Pediatric Society" [6] in 1914, a physician recommends removal of adhesions of the clitoris in the case of female infants inclined to masturbation. "These [adhesions] may be separated without the use of an anesthetic," he writes, adding: "The operation under these conditions is very painful." Just why no anesthetic need be used is not explained, but one finds a hint of explanation in a subsequent statement: "In several cases circumcision and the removal of adenoids at the same time effected a complete cure."

Since the lips and mouth are an erogenous center very important to the young child, this simultaneous punishment of two pleasure zones instead of one was surely a stroke of genius. The mother probably had a very easy disciplinary time thereafter, having only to suggest to the little girl that they "go see the doctor."

Removal of the ovaries does not remove sexual desire, for the pituitary gland helps out with hormone production and the nerve endings of the erogenous centers persist. Removal of the clitoris was also a failure, since the surface of that area continued to be supplied with nerve endings. Even with congenital absence of the clitoris, writes Dr. Dickinson, "The friction evidences are outstanding in Bell's and in my two cases," [7] suggesting that erotic propensities remained.

CHAPTER TWELVE

education for frigidity

*We must not forget that humanity, oppressed by
its sexual needs, is prepared to accept anything, if
only the "overcoming of sexuality" is held out as
bait.*

SIGMUND FREUD

Sex behavior requires some sort of behavior; the sex
act requires activity. The physiology of sex, hormones and glands are often spoken of. We hear
much of the delivery system in which woman plays
a receptive role and man a mercurial. We understand some of the complicated psychological attach-
ments and pathic fixations with which humans
enter the nuptial scene.

But our question is simpler. If the sex act is an
act, what type of act is it? Is sex behavior an in-
destructible unit of motor reaction born into the
child (the male child) and ready for performance
the moment reproductive maturity is reached? Can
man be counted on to carry out this function with
uniformity and aplomb? The bewilderment that
typically surrounds the human nuptial would indicate otherwise—that appropriate organs, physiological processes, and psychic communion may be
present, but the sexual adjustment far from rewarding, or even discoverable.

The humble ant has an easier time. It leaps at

birth into its caste position in society as worker, soldier, or whatever life provides. Only a few ants have a reproductive tradition to uphold, and these make their routine adjustment independent of previous experience or social pressure. If an ant is isolated from its fellows, it does not turn poet or philosopher but remains what it is: a caste-constituted soldier, worker, lover.

The primate family finds all sexual-social adjustments more complicated. This is due to the gap between birth and maturity, a time-elapse which becomes more pronounced as one clambers up the evolutionary tree. Man has the most endless childhood of all, a time fraught with rewards and punishments, directions and maldirections. He learns the hard way.

Among primates, monkeys have the briefest wait till maturity. Their sexual adjustments consequently display more precision and are closer to an instinctual level. With monkeys there is little individual difference in the way the sex adjustment is made. Behavior is more uniform, exact, and unhesitating. With a higher primate like the chimpanzee, whose childhood occupies eight or nine years and rivals the human in this respect, adult sexual adjustments become increasingly variegated.

Individual chimpanzees assume quite different attitudes toward sex. One chimpanzee will be hurried, expressionless, intense, brief. Another animal is leisurely, smiling, exploratory, playful. Still another, brought up in isolation and presented with his first opportunity to mate, responded with puzzlement, made a few ineffective tries and failed. This last chimpanzee lacked neither hormones, sensory centers, nor a desirable object. The behavioral pattern was lacking.

Over a period of years Dr. H. C. Bingham observed the sex development of a group of laboratory chimpanzees. As the young animals grew, day after day, week after week, year after year, they began to display various types of behavior, motor responses and play habits, characteristic of young primates: chasing, clinging, pulling, tumbling, strutting, fleeing, teasing, petting, romping, eating, fighting, and tantrums. Whether any of these behavioral patterns would prove significant for later sexual development remained to be seen.

The appearance of a sexual concomitant in these activities was very simply noted. With the romping or the fighting or the strutting or fleeing, a temporary erection might occur, either in male or female, or brief evidence of pelvic thrusts or presentation-patterns. These ordinary play activities, while non-sexual in their inception, proved directly relevant to later reproductive adjustments.

"It seems probable," writes Bingham, "that specific sexual practices grow out of a diffused mass of individual and social phenomena in which necessary reaction patterns for the full functioning of copulation are practiced and perfected in the absence of any certain sexual focus, and when the copulatory situation arises the adjustment is in large part a rehearsal of former activities." [1]

Bingham stressed the fact that sexual responses did not by any means occupy the entire play time of the chimpanzees. Among his total observations, sex behavior was displayed only one to five percent of the time. A young and immature chimpanzee might wrestle with a companion, show evidence of erotic stirrings, and then roll casually aside to concentrate on a piece of fruit or someone swinging, oblivious to the fact that he had been exposed to (what humans would regard as) an opportunity.

Since the chimpanzees' adult sexual adjustments develop out of the non-sexual behavioral patterns of childhood, we may find here a key to the prevalent maladjustments of humans. Differential play patterns can account for much of the incompatibility between the sexes. For clinging, tumbling, chasing, and romping there is a generally acknowledged need present in a child. Yet before an American infant is out of the crib, it is being taught to express this need in one direction rather than in another, depending entirely upon its sex. If one examines the diverse cultural backgrounds from which men and women emerge, one is surprised to find as much congeniality as does exist in this typical marriage of a Confucian tradition with a Promethean one.

The Social Embrace

Of the five senses, the sense of touch is most nearly perfected at birth. Children are extremely responsive to pressure contacts. They like to be held, carried, and played with. The young chimpanzee exhibits this same basic need, finding reassurance and pleasure in contact with others. Bingham describes it in this way, "In response to manual pressure by humans or by their own kind, the young animals learn to adjust much as a man in the chair of a barber."

The variety of pressure contacts which the human young receive will differ from one culture to the next, and from one family to the next. This helps account for differences in cultures and differences in family traditions. What is important for our discussion is that pressure contacts *within* a culture differ according to the sex of the child. If a different species of pressure contact is characteristically awarded male and female, it might explain the emergence of a bi-sexual pattern of adult preference.

Every pressure contact that is not disagreeable establishes some small hope of renewal. If a touch is pleasant, one has hopes of its recurring. Upon sufficient repetitions, and recurrent sensory rewards, the flexible organism develops expectations, desires, and a preference for one type of experience rather than another. If at the moment of a pleasurable pressure contact, severe or mild-but-persistent punishment descends from some outside force such as a parent, the pressure contact will have less tendency to develop any enthusiasm about recurring. A pleasant pressure contact is easily outvoted by an irate parent.

In this way a culture is able to guide the expectations and hopes and desires of its inmates. In our culture one type of preference is reinforced in the girl, and another in the boy. What's more, these preferences are to a great extent antithetical.

Even in the first months of life there is a tendency to treat females with more gentleness than males. The tradition of caressing baby girls and jouncing baby boys is widespread, though this sheep-and-goats training is not so pronounced until the child is out of the crib and into its distinctive dress

and romper. The child of three or six or ten does
not lose its love of pressure contacts. Like its simian
cousin, it continues to like to touch and be touched.
Even at this tender age, the child discovers that in
the inexorable logic of grownups certain pressure
contacts are permissible while others are not. What
classification of pressure contact is allowed, and
their hierarchical arrangement, depends somewhat
on the family but mostly on the sex of the child.

Approved pressure contacts for girls are kissing,
fondling, and being tossed gently into the air. Con-
versely, pressure contacts approved for boys are wrestling, tackling, and slapping one another on the
back. "Aren't boys rough!" parents exclaim hope-
fully. "Isn't she sweet!"—of sister.

The behavioral pattern required of young girls
stresses moderation, receptivity, kindliness. The
boy is inoculated with Promethean bustle, a need
for perpetual, reckless activity and the display of
power. His movements are expected to be abrupt,
efficient, egotistic, and unsentimental. On entering
marriage he automatically attempts to establish a
sexual adjustment that will do justice to his tradition and is surprised that any alternative cultural
pattern should exist. The girl, therefore, is apt to
find the tender mooning atmosphere of courtship
abruptly replaced by an energetic species of exercise,
a form of physical involvement that differs completely from the sweet hesitancies she has learned
to expect of love.

Women do not often recognize that courtship
is a phase in which the preferences of women are ri-
tualistically catered to: the wooing is a preliminary
concession to those pressure contacts women love—

gentleness, tenderness, kissing, caressing. With marriage comes a startling change of events, the woman's preferences being set aside in favor of the duties of marriage, the preferences of the husband. The man has heroically fulfilled the role of suitor, onerous though it may have been, and now considers it his right to indulge in his own preferred types of pressure contact, learned on the playing field. The sex booklets, which at this point recommend that the husband continue a routine deference to the woman's preferences (foreplay), are treating the symptom rather than the cause.

Poor old Nature, who so often has referred back to her just such a mismated pair and is expected after twenty years of adverse conditioning to promote a unity of opinion! In spite of Nature's gifts to the sexes of similar sensory and hormonic equipment, and of similar impulses toward communal play, Society has managed to step in and indoctrinate these sweet and affectionate animals with opposite conceptions of what is love.

The Hostility of the Sexes
or
Sugar and Spice vs. Snakes and Snails

At an early age a girl is given a doll with an imaginary skin which she holds and cares for. A deep interest in textures, the interior decoration of the home, her own clothes, her doll's clothes is encouraged. She is taught various occupations around the house, most of them requiring caution, care, and extraordinary manual precision. She learns to dry fragile china and glasses at an age when boys

are supposed to be breaking the furniture. She is
taught the rules of propriety: a table is set in a certain way, the salad plate goes on this spot and the
spoon on that. Indoors, the conventional rites of
society take on a grave importance. The girl receives
an almost Oriental education in considerateness,
modesty, social custom, filial piety, and flower arrangement.

This training automatically punishes her for opposite sorts of activity. She is ridiculed for being a
tomboy, or categorically forbidden rough sports. She
is to keep clean and remain dignified—sometimes at
the age of three. All sensory needs are expected to
fulfill themselves through socially approved modes of
pressure contact, kissing and hugging being first
on the list. The girl develops a diffuse erogenous
glow, a kind of St. Elmo's fire, and avoids any sharply
localized erotic spark.

Meanwhile the young boy, later transmitter of
the Total Responsibility Theory, is outdoors developing as rough a nature as his parents can afford. If
he is discovered running his hand over a piece of
satin, there is concern lest he develop into a sissy.
For discovering just such a sensory reward, the little
girl will be congratulated, "Yes, *isn't* it nice, dear!"

In sharp contrast to the soft-treaded strolling and
the contactless jumping rope of girls, a boy practices thrusts and tackling, tumbling and exertion.
The American boy's youth involves one of the most
exhausting programs of competitive sports devised
since the days of Sparta. He is bullied into keeping
on the move just as much as the girl is startled into
quiescence. Since roughness affords pleasure, and
society forbids gentle contacts, he rapidly learns

to eschew feminine kisses and caresses from his mother or others, and prefers to be out on the gridiron tackling his chums. His desire for caress is one thing that makes the little boy so rough.

While the boy's acquaintance is with rough textures, grass and earth, land and sea, extremes of hot and cold, fair weather and foul, we say to the girl child: the greatest joy of your animal childhood is to sit in a little room of your own with pink curtains at the window and blue rabbits on the wall, with a miniature stove and Frigidaire finished in white enamel, and to play dolls and "play."

If a mother discovers her young son and daughter wrestling, she usually feels there is something vaguely indecent about it. Even though the little girl may on this occasion have established a half-nelson and be about to pin her brother to the ground, the mother's injunction will be the same: "Junior! Don't hurt Joan! You know girls aren't as strong as you!" As the children get shamefully to their feet, obedient to their mother's note of horror (and it *was* pleasurable), Joan really believes she was about to be hurt in some uncalculated way, and Junior thinks he was about to forget his strength and wound a lady. Already pleasure begins to smack of the harmful.

Two other minor but essential factors in adult sexual adjustment may appear strangely distasteful to the girl: the minimum uncovering that is required and the character of the reproductive secretions, both well-known to the boy long before marriage. Uncovering is a familiar thing to him, and it has positive connotations from early training. Nor is the viscosity of the seminal fluid a surprise to the boy, who has generally learned to take pride in exactly this. Yet both these trivial and inescapable factors of sex may appear alien and even repugnant to a girl who discovers their existence for the first time.

Is she not taught that her own secretions are objectionable? Suddenly she is expected to submit to or even approve the more ample secretions of reproduction. Her experiences in life have singled out for approval only what was "clean." As homemaker and housekeeper she was taught to approve only what was immaculate, free from moisture, and related to the textile family. She always stayed indoors and kept her feet dry when her little brother played football on the marshy ground. She stood by and watched when he sailed his boat or plunged his hands into the water to retrieve it.

As to modesty, it is the immemorial possession of her sex, a privilege, and at first all ten commandments rolled into one. Of all the features of reproduction, the one that shocks a small child the most is probably the news that a certain uncovering is required. A mother may tell a child that people have to kiss each other, or love each other, in order to have children. But both mother and child know that the worst part of it is that the people are somewhat unclothed. Nothing more than this blow to modesty is needed to understand the classic tears of the child in the following story.

The little girl arrived home one evening and poked a mournful head into the living room. "Mother, will you hear my prayers tonight?" The mother went upstairs presently and found the little girl sitting up in bed. "What is it, dear?" "I went out with Edna," *sob*, "and Edna said that babies . . . !"

She ended in a crescendo: "Did you and *Daddy* have to do *that?*" The mother searched her mind nervously for the right reassurance. "But darling," she said finally, "if we hadn't done that, why, you and Johnny wouldn't be here!" "You mean," the child wailed, "you had to do it *twice?*"

The Division of Labor

When Promethean man and Confucian woman, like two species of plant, set up housekeeping together, their tastes and preferences are expected to supplement one another in the most agreeable fashion. Man is assigned sway over the World, while woman is given charge of kitchen, nursery, and the physical (not the conversational) upkeep of the living room. In sexual adjustments the woman is to be receptive and the man propulsive. It sounds beautiful on paper.

But women complain of persistent frustrations and of frigidity in particular. It is time to examine the components of adult sexuality to see what it is women have lost along the way. Sex adjustment requires the use of sensory centers; at least one of these is peremptorily tabooed. Sex adjustment requires hormones; present. Sex also has a behavioral element; it requires an act. If so, who acts? If sensory nerves are useless without constantly changing pressure, who directs these pressures? If a choice in pressure contacts is involved, whose choice and what contacts? If sex activity is purposeful, answering to the needs of the organism, whose purpose and whose organism?

The Total Responsibility Theory has one answer

for all these questions. It is the man who acts, he
who chooses what species of pressure contact is
employed, his organism which possesses the needs
to be answered. The Theory benevolently informs
the man that his own preferences automatically answer the preferences of the woman. No wonder
hostility of the sexes sometimes develops.

While men, we admit, rule the world of business
and art, inter-family and international affairs, women
we do not admit rule the world of the home. Even a
woman's complaints, from which comes her reputation as a termagant, are often the vocal exercise
and protest of someone who is not actually being
listened to. In a canvass made during a recent elec-
tion, a group of husbands were asked if they ever
discussed politics with their wives; most of them
said no. Their wives were asked the same question,
if they ever discussed politics with their husbands,
and answered yes. It was the women who were under
the delusion that there had been an exchange of
ideas.

That America is a matriarchy because women take
the family purse to market and don't have to laugh
at their husbands' jokes is only a small part of the
story. In the invisible but nonetheless significant
realm of sex an unchallenged patriarchy still holds.

CHAPTER THIRTEEN

the laws of rapture

Love, to Whom necessity is play
W. H. AUDEN

The sympathetic nervous system is not particularly concerned with the conceptual life of man. It is more interested in actual than contemplated acts, and reserves a special affection for man's major emotions, the excitements of the flesh. Since the sympathetic nervous system is the haven of excitement, it is also the home of sexual gratification. It controls the muscular contractions of orgasm.

If this sympathetic system were wholly accessible to the will, we would have no more sexual complaints about the hostility of the body toward decisions of the mind. As it is, man cannot by mental effort control the contractions of the prostate, tubes, and uterus or induce orgasm, any more than he can accelerate the heart, dilate the pupils of the eye, or shift the blood from one region to another.

To the extent that one can invent a strong emotion through mental images, one can stimulate the sympathetic system and force it to gain momentum. This is not so easy, especially if a major emotion is to be invented. Try to produce a genuine rage in yourself; it takes a good deal of skill.

Nor can the sympathetic nervous system be fooled by reasonable facsimiles. Excitement must come to it as a spontaneous impulse. Presented with a scintillating but counterfeit emotion, the sympathetic system cuts it dead like a hypocritical friend. There are multiple occasions for excitement in life, however, and it is largely a matter of avoiding their expungement. We have seen that women are forbidden behavioral expression in many ways. Can it be they are also forbidden excitement?

Orgasm requires intense excitement and the cooperation of the sympathetic nervous system. The body is a wheel that, once stimulated, proves self-accelerating. Excitement has an energizing effect. The sympathetic system is stimulated by excitement and creates further excitement. The culmination of this process, sexually, is orgasm.

What happens in women? Why does excitement so often die down, cease to accumulate momentum, and stop short of orgasm?

The answer goes back to a physiological fact. Excitement increases *motor* (*muscular*) *efficiency*. Strong excitement automatically drives the blood from the vegetative organs, such as the stomach, to the organs needed for muscular exertion—the lungs, heart, and central nervous system. When blood is rushed to the skeletal muscles, the body becomes poised for action.[1]

But action, or any inclination to act or take initiative, is forbidden women. Motor efficiency in sex is the prerogative of man. Thus an excitement which might give rise to an activity that is tabooed will find itself in turn discouraged. This is true in all realms—social, political, and economic. Where society frowns on initiative, it frowns on the excitement that induces this initiative.[2] Hence the discourage-

ment of certain types of political excitement or "agitation."

The excitements which lead to the motor
efficiency called war are properly discouraged.
Society would do well to eliminate the "excitements" leading to race hatred. But women have a
right to protest against their own motor efficiency in
the realm of love being included in this list of social
enemies.

Further, if excitement is not allowed to accumulate, there is little possibility of orgasm. We will find
that the motor efficiency of women is generally eval-
uated in terms of how much pleasure it gives men.

How Women Manage to be Frigid and
Over-Emotional

While women are commonly regarded as sexually
frigid, it is equally traditional to regard them as extremely emotional. The word *emotion* originally
meant strong feeling or agitation, but it has been
modified by usage until it fits like a glove the mild
unsatisfied longings of women. Emotion, to accommodate this nebulous feminine world, has taken on
a meaning of diffuseness and internal vibration. It
is, so to say, an Excitement from which the intensity and motor efficiency have been removed.

No wonder Eros, in its more physical manifestations, has taken men to its bosom rather than
women. The wheel of the body and the laws of rapture gain mobility in men. They acquire the
swiftness and efficiency of a Silver Meteor, while in
women the same processes, beset by bit and rein,

slow down to the monotonous pace of a one-horse
shay.

If the realm of sex is reserved for men, when are
women allowed to act, to carry out motor responses,
manipulate the environment, execute tasks, initiate
deeds? Women have a great deal to accomplish.
They must win a husband, wash dishes, cook, clean,
and nurse the sick, they must bear children, discipline them, shop for a new hat, demand fidelity of a
husband, slave after beauty, invite flattery, and in a
negative escape-movement express active fear of the
dark, the cold, the opposite sex, and mice.

This is Woman's World. It is here that we find
her earning the title of emotionality. Since these
matters, chiefly domestic, wholly feminine, strike
men as being of somewhat indifferent concern—not
in their total effect, but in their detail—women's
emotion is often called emotionalism. When one
does not find the motor efficiency of an individual
of much consequence, one depreciates the excitements that inspire it. Men benefit from women's ca-
pability in cooking and nursing, but they do not for
a moment put this motor efficiency on a par with
the motor efficiency of Joe DiMaggio or the work of
fatherhood.

A woman need not hesitate to become intensely
excited over a trousseau, her child's first step, somebody's health, a recipe, a husband's faux pas, crows-
feet around the eyes, or the presence of a small gray
mouse. In these proverbial excitements a woman
has carte blanche. The wedding day may interest a
woman more than the wedding night, which can
frighten her a little, and quite rightly: it is the realm
of male dominance. The world of the home excites

women more than the world of politics, which requires the behavioral responses of men and is likely to get muddled if women interfere.

So it goes. We find that women are forbidden intense excitement in any realm in which their behavioral response is not desired. And their behavioral response has a peculiar way of being excluded from those realms in which men enjoy traditional priority. Women can become efficient in womanly pursuits, for these by definition do not compete with male prestige.

When some new and unprecedented field requiring motor efficiency comes into being, as with the invention of the typewriter and the automobile, there is a certain trial period in which medical and mechanical authorities—all male—discuss whether women are strong enough to handle the new instruments. This seriously took place in the case of the typewriter. What eventually happened was that men woke up to the fact that the typewriter, that infernal machine, while at first interesting and novel, was actually extremely tedious to operate, and they forthwith handed it over to the world of women whom they have never ceased to congratulate for their dexterity and precision in regard to it. The automobile proved to be much more fun, and became a machine only susceptible to the motor efficiency of men, who erected a barrier of jokes to exclude women drivers from their new toy.

Free Wheeling

"Excitement—revealed by romping, teasing, petting, fleeing, eating, fighting, tantrums, and com-

monly by mixtures of these and other activities—
was a consistent forerunner of sexual responses,"
writes Bingham of the chimpanzees. There is little
of a consistent nature in the behavior of these
variable animals, and the fact that excitement-
associated-with-certain-behavior [8] was present in all
sexual responses is significant. Excitement is not
only a preliminary but an accompaniment of sex.

The wheels of rapture turn most briskly for
women during courtship, when chivalry is in flower
and women with their indoor preferences in the
game are being approached tenderly and apprecia-
tively by the earnest male. Women have a real function then, and they revel in it. The feminine qualities
of modesty and beauty seem at the moment more
powerful than the masculine virtues of enterprise
and courage. The ardent suitor adopts the very picture of deference.

In courtship, beauty and modesty are allowed to
try their strength, to demonstrate their own motor
efficiency before saying goodbye to a proud world in
favor of the T.R.T. If success results, success being
marriage, the woman has won the chief victory of
her life. Sexually her triumphs are over. Praise is no
longer reserved for her attractiveness as a woman,
but for the way she takes care of her husband, his
house and children. Only in respect to these is excitement allowed to develop, and to find behavioral
outlet.

Even here the man is apt to neglect her efforts,
for he was never very attentive to indoor life. No
wonder a woman turns up a little hysterically at
afternoon bridge, where she comes in contact with
people from a similar cultural background, indoors.

They too emerged from a steamheated island called home, and share her excitement over the price of breadfruit. They can sympathize with her habitual concern over propriety, beauty, nuances, and duty.

During the wooing, a woman reflects, it was *her* acts, *her* decisions, that mattered. It was her excitements, her preferred forms of pressure-contact, her yeses and her noes that took precedence and attracted attention. After marriage she must take care that her own excitements do not contradict or interrupt those of her husband. In constantly reminding herself that his needs are more important than hers, she finds it simpler to reduce excitements to *sympathetic emotions*, rather than risk letting them multiply into ecstatic demands.

She sometimes misses her old privilege of exclaiming, *Oh no! please!* The *Oh no!* tradition in women offers a secret sense of participation in a matter in which they really have no business whatever, beyond consent. *Oh no!*—it reminds a woman that for the moment her own motor responses are terribly interesting to the man. Perhaps the nefarious teaser only wants to prolong this happiness. *Oh no!* fulfills her obligation of modesty and unwillingness, and yet gives a sense of active participation, if only in a delaying action.

After marriage, when the T.R.T. takes over the love relationship quietly and inexorably, her motor responses are of less concern. It is up to her to submit, express gratitude and omit complaint. But she can't help sighing over it all, and reminding her husband of the other suitors she had and how she might have chosen one of them and still be saying *Oh no! please!*—to her husband. When sympathetic

emotion took the place of courtship excitement, the
woman moved farther away from the factors involved in orgasm than she was before.

> Her tiny feet
> Like snails did creep
> A little out, and then
> As if they started at bo-peep
> Did soon draw in again.
>
> —HERRICK

The enemy of excitement is Fatigue. Laboratory
experiments have shown that while resting will reduce fatigue only after an hour or more, the release
of adrenalin will accomplish this rejuvenation in five
minutes or less.[4] Unfortunately, it is excitement
which stimulates the adrenal glands to secrete
adrenalin. Exertion and "behavior" activates the
sympathetic nervous system and promotes excitement. Excitement activates the sympathetic nervous
system and promotes exertion. Excitement (in sex),
exertion, and behavior are forbidden the female.

No wonder women complain of feeling tired.

Excitement produces various fervent effects: acceleration of the heart, rapid respiration, dilated pupils, pallor or flushing. Yet any manifestation of
these in a female is regarded with horror, as a breath
from the grave. The little girl is taught to guard
against any "strain" being put on her system. A
boy's pallor over a basketball game is attributed to
his excitement over which side will win. The same
pallor in a girl indicates that she is about to faint.
No wonder she often does.

Women are bewildered because their first response to sex is so prompt, spontaneous and rewarding. Up to a point excitement prevails. But suddenly something in them *stops climbing.* Pleasure retreats. They feel tired, exhausted, they don't want any more. Taught to avoid any "strain" on their system, the intolerable excitements of sex become terrifying, paralyzing.

Go ahead and *love!* we say to women. But don't get so excited about it!

When a woman begins to speed toward a climax, she is likely to hear a siren in her ears and her mother's voice saying, Pull over to the curb, dear, you're driving too fast.

It is the woman, who is not required to "do anything" in the sex act, who usually suffers the most from fatigue. Women do nothing and get tired doing it. This becomes comprehensible with an understanding of the energizing effect of excitement and spontaneous exertion. It is precisely because women do nothing that they get so tired doing it. The cure is not rest and sedatives but the freedom to participate.

What is frequent in unhappy sexual relations? Fatigue. What can relieve fatigue? Adrenalin. What stimulates adrenalin? Excitement. Who is the notorious Tired One of marriages? The woman. For whom is excitement supposed dangerous? She!

Women need excitement. They need the energy and freedom of excitement, a capacity with which they were born, but which has been systematically drained out of them on the ground that they cannot stand what boys can. It is excitement and spontaneity that can dissolve the fears that women bring to marriage. Instead they are expected to conquer shame by brain-waves, psychoanalysis, "receptivity," thoughts of childbearing.

A boy learns in games to carry on beyond an initial point of fatigue. Excitement is healthy, he is told; it is nothing to be ashamed of. The phenomenon of second wind is nothing more than the victory of excitement over fatigue. An enthusiasm which refuses to be downed stimulates the release of adrenalin and literally cures fatigue. The least suggestion of fatigue in a woman appears to her as just retribution for her wickedness. She has allowed herself to become excited, there has been an accumulation of muscle tone—which is in itself improper in a female, and what her mother always predicted has come about: her body has broken down in the midst of things.

Sexual excitement does not tire women. It is their fight against it that proves so wearying. Instead of the rewards of energy, joy, and physiological satisfaction, the frigid woman experiences fear, emotional blockage, and frustration. Fatigue has an easy time gaining ascendancy over joy as long as excitement is in disrepute with her body.

Women are expected to keep control of themselves. Their hysteria is an excitement that finds no permissible outlet. Men stamp out of the house; women stay home and have hysterics. Hysteria involves maximum exertion with minimum motor efficiency. It is excitement stymied, excitement in search of expression, excitement revealing itself as impotent and self-frustrating. It helps demonstrate to men that they have nothing to fear.

A woman struggling away from her own frigidity tries everything—everything but an examination of her own wishes. She tries willpower, she tries cosmic responsiveness, she tries transference and sublimation, she tries self-castigation, concealment, she tries unwillingness. *Oh no! please!*—it is all that's left to show she is a free being in a free environment making a free choice. Maybe she is lucky in this much, for it is more than most minorities are permitted.

Unlearning Frigidity

The problems of unlearning are somewhat different from those of learning. There are still the twin propulsions, reward and punishment, which have to be weighed against each other. If a habit becomes totally unsatisfactory, it is always and easily exchanged for another. An old and established habit, however, is bound to have an aura of reward. Why was the habit adopted in the first place if it did not offer some reward? A neurotic impulse is one that hesitates to relinquish a small and familiar reward although mountainous frustrations may have gathered around the habit as a whole.

The habit of frigidity at first offers rewards to a woman. When she was a child, such symptoms won her the approval of her mother. Now that she is an adult, it wins her a husband's love. For if he believes a woman should be seen and not heard, frigidity fills the bill. If he worries lest he not satisfy her, frigidity combined with expressions of gratitude restores his self-confidence. Frigidity is only in disrepute when it becomes known. To omit complaints, to proclaim one's love, to smile among one's neighbors: how is frigidity to be detected then? Many marriages start

out with the woman clutching fervently at these
reward factors: the inexpressible satisfaction of
thinking of oneself as normal and average and of
trouble to nobody.

These early rewards of social conformity become
less important in succeeding years. At any rate, the
wife and mother is likely to become aware that
something is missing in the biological realm. Yet by
this late date, any change of habit seems to threaten
the structure of the marriage. Unlearning a habit,
particularly a pervasive habit like frigidity, will have
repercussions. That the cure of frigidity only requires a tacit decision on the part of the woman to
be more feminine and responsive henceforward is
sanguine in the extreme.

How is neurosis in other fields resolved? How are
unsatisfactory habits banished? Dr. Jules H. Masserman studied the relative effectiveness of various
types of therapy—by first producing neurotic symptoms in a bevy of laboratory cats. A hungry cat was
placed in a cage that contained a box. When a light
flashed on, it signalled to the cat that food could be
obtained from the box. The cat learned to proceed
to the box only after receiving the light-signal. No
sooner had the animal grown used to this pleasant
sequence of events, settling down in the best Main
Street manner, than the investigator played a trick
of fate.

Cats do not favor blasts of air. As the light flashed
on and the hungry cat came confidently to the box
and attempted to feed, an airblast was shot across
the box. An airblast will not kill a cat, but considering how hungry the animal was and how sharp its
expectations, this villainous plot was disillusioning

to its nerve centers. The cat's habits had led it to expect a pure and unadulterated reward from the box.
It received punishment. The light-signal began to
mean intense reward and intense punishment, min-
gled. It attracted the cat toward the box and im-
pelled it to retreat. The cat developed neurotic
symptoms of fear, indecision, and conflict. It was
hungry but would not go near the box containing
food.

Thus even a dumb brute, wanting discourse of
reason, can acquire neurosis—until it starves in the
sight of food, remains imprisoned in sight of escape,
and trembles in the presence of safety. Having produced neurotic symptoms in the cats, the investigator proceeded to study ways and means of reducing
or abolishing the neurosis. He tried rest, reassurance, force, and other therapies used for human
neurosis.

A cure frequently attempted in women frightened
by sex is rest, temporary removal from the situation
inducing fear. In the experiment with the cats, however, rest was not particularly satisfactory. After
months of rest, the symptoms eased only slightly,
while one return to the feared situation, a single
blast of air, and the neurosis reinstated itself virtually in full force.

In all therapy the proposed solution should be
levelled at relieving the symptoms of the victim
rather than at making life easier for her husband or
friends. To inform an hysterical woman that her cure
lies in relaxing, or being more responsive, is to urge
her to drug her symptoms rather than discover the
cause.

Another typical treatment of frigidity is reassur-

ance. In the cat's dilemma, one of the experiment-
ers might take the animal to the food box and encourage it to eat. This is the role assigned to the
husband. However, the test of whether an action is
reassuring or not lies entirely in its effect on the patient. If the patient does not feel reassured, reassurance is not taking place, regardless of how much
effort and self-sacrifice the husband is putting into
it. If a cat did not happen to trust the experimenter
who purported to reassure it, this method was in-
effectual. If reassurance actually took place, it slowly
relieved the neurotic symptoms.

Force is another method, currently discredited,
for solving neurosis. It operates widely in the form
of social pressure. In testing this method, a cat was
forced toward the box it feared by a movable wall in
its cage. Finally arriving in the vicinity of the box,
which now contained "delectable pellets of salmon
seasoned with catnip," driven inwardly by intense
hunger, the cat would often overcome its fear and
begin to eat rapidly and compulsively.

This method of reducing anxiety would be extremely difficult to reproduce in the human realm.
Food hunger is not subject to the delightful subli-
mations that sexual hunger is. The human
affections find rewards in symbols, and in textures,
epicurism, exercise, and all sorts of contacts. It
would therefore be difficult to insure maximum
need or hunger in the woman to be cured by this
means. Furthermore, a cat has had years of happy
eating experience, which serves as an invisible incen-
tive. It is not so with women and sex.

A fourth type of therapy was to feed the cat before placing it in the cage, thus reducing its hunger

and easing the intensity of the conflict. If the animal began to starve itself rather than approach the food box, the investigator tried satisfying its hunger somewhat, before subjecting it to its old terror. When this was done, the neurotic symptoms were "significantly less marked." Women in many ways instinctively seek partial satisfaction of their affections by way of lessening marital fears. We do not know, in fact, how often self-orgasm is employed as a means of promoting diminution of the intensity of the conflictful hunger drive, to ease anxiety.

Optimum Moments of Her Own Selection

The most interesting therapy involved a distinguished group of cats who were trained not merely to respond to the flash of light but to act in producing it. This reminds us of the different groups in society, some of whom are expected to respond to flashes of light controlled by others and those privileged groups who attend to the flashing. The cats belonging to the latter group obtained food by themselves manipulating the switch that controlled both the feeding signals (the light) and the automatic deposition of food in the box. When they succeeded with the switch, they were rewarded—by food; when they failed, they were punished, for no food appeared.

Having become proficient in this partial control of their environment, these cats resisted neurosis longer than their "responsive" brethren did. The conflict awakened by the airblast did not throw them into conniptions as readily as it did their feline fellows, although the latter were actually liv-

ing on a more primitive, less symbolic level; which is
thought to promote stability and repose. The happy
slaves of the light signal, then, who had nothing to
do but respond when the flash came, were more
quickly unseated by the airblast.

Even the cats with manipulative habits finally got
upset over the airblast occurring whenever they
wanted food, and they began to avoid the switch
and develop symptoms of anxiety. As their hunger
grew, however, these cats—instead of moping
around all day—experimentally returned to the
switch, and *in spite of repetitions of the airblast*
finally reestablished their feeding patterns. A
clear-cut victory of spontaneity over serfdom!
"These neurotic animals, then," writes Dr. Masserman, " 'worked through' their conflict in a manner
denied to others not given the partial manipulative
control of the experimental situation." [5]

This therapeutic device, requiring the behavioral
participation of the animal, proved useful to the unhappy cat. Yet this type of therapy is blankly forbidden women in the solution of their problems. Anything but initiative, is the advice, anything but an
infringement of the T.R.T. Women are given reassurance, they are provided with rest; they can exert
will power, they are experimentally called abnormal,
they are bullied and cajoled. The one thing society
will not discuss is the possibility of giving them freedom with which to seek an excitement and behavioral expression that will, through trial and error, resolve their frustrations.

No greater danger to satisfactory adjustment for
women exists than the pervasive social view that
women are automatically dependent on the motor

activities of men, that women can solve their anxieties only by a solemn responsiveness to light signals manipulated by others. The cat with the most spectacular recovery and resilience was one who worked-through its problems "until, through trial activity at optimum moments of its own selection, it had spontaneously resolved its motivational conflicts and dissipated the 'neurosis.'"

It is not that the Total Responsibility Theory should be taken out of the hands of men and put into the hands of women, or that an egotistic drive for self-satisfaction should struggle for dominance between man and woman. Any suggested change of habitual patterns is discredited by translating it into an extreme. All that is required is for women to be occasionally allowed to choose optimum moments, when spontaneity and confidence seem at a height, in which to resolve some of the more serious and persistent conflicts known to their sex.

CHAPTER FOURTEEN

women as something special

Let Husbands Know,
Their wives have sense like them: They see, and smell,
And have their Palates both for sweet, and sour,
As Husbands have.

EMILIA, in *Othello*

How can rights for men and women be equal? Men and women are different, and their rights will be different, not equal or unequal. "Freedom is a man's word," writes D. H. Lawrence; "its meaning, to a woman, is really rather trivial." And he adds sadly, "Woman is truly less free today than ever she has been since time began, in the womanly sense of freedom. Which means, she has less peace, less of that lovely womanly peace that flows like a river, less of the lovely, flower-like repose of a happy woman, less of the nameless joy in life, purely unconscious, which is the very breath of a woman's being."

Why speak of menial worldly equalities in connection with these unique creatures? "Let us but ascend to the first snows of the mountain," Maeterlinck tells us, "and all inequalities are levelled by the purifying hand of the horizon that opens before us." Women balance man's loftiest thoughts with small words spoken of silver bangles and trinkets of glass. Women are nearer to the mysteries; they have communications with the unknown.

Maeterlinck was not arguing against equal rights; he was trying to explain why women were superior to men. For it is women who "preserve here below the pure fragrance of our soul, like some jewel from Heaven."

Lawrence echoed this deification, describing woman as "a living fountain whose spray falls delicately around her, on all that come near." He reserved this metaphor for "real women" only, as could be expected. Any woman who expressed an opinion instead of acting like a well-behaved fountain fell under the Lawrencian bombast.

What a relief it is to turn to the candor and the cruelty of a Nietzsche who gave women the compliment of treating them as an equal, albeit an enemy. Parodying Goethe's eternally feminine, Nietzsche exclaims, "Alas, if ever the 'eternally tedious in woman'—she has plenty of it! is allowed to venture forth!" And mocking the Lawrence and Maeterlinck versions he makes the peculiarly feminist comment: "Woman has hitherto been treated by men like birds, which, losing their way, have come down among them from an elevation: as something delicate, fragile, wild, strange, sweet, and animating—but as something also which must be cooped up to prevent it flying away."

There are two traps on the route to equal rights for women. One is the deification trap: woman is promised protection and reward if she will adopt the traditional deference attitudes toward men. The other trap is a maze of logic, in which the enjoyment of differences between men and women, and between individual women, is replaced by a sudden deification of "real" women, that vast majority who are thought to prefer the kitchen to anything else. In the course of a congenial syllogism, the tremblesome minority who were going to be permitted to be exceptions, or have careers, are lost along the way, having dropped through the trap door reserved for suspicious characters.

In his book, *The Coming American Fascism*, Lawrence Dennis employs both these traps, coaxing women into the warm friendly kitchen of fascism and then in an aside to the audience explaining that this environment will always be most pleasing for persons with the peculiar physical and spiritual limitations of women. "Men and women are different, not equal or unequal to each other," Dennis writes.

"No reasonable fascist will deny," he continues, apparently having someone in mind, that a few women will achieve desirable values outside the home. But as in many quasi-liberal theses today, we have not travelled far before we discover that the careers to which women will have full access under fascism are "employment for which a man would not be suitable, such, for instance, as a chorus girl or a matron in a woman's institution."

That this harbinger of order and uniformity was violently opposed to feminism we are happy to note. "Feminism says that women are just folks. Fascism says that they are women. The feminists may want to be legal persons, but most women, who are feminine rather than feminists, prefer to be women."

Women who really want to be women will act

like women!—this is a current version of the same
thing, with the usual psychoanalytic rumblings. In a
short declarative sentence we are actually presented
with three different definitions for the same word.
Let us bob into the dissecting room for a moment.

Women who really want to be WOMEN will act like
WOMEN.

This first Women is all of us, you and I, your
wife, sister, and mother. It is the individual woman
with all her fears and hopes and imperfections.
WOMEN—but this second women only includes normal women. If you aren't a normal woman, please
raise your right hand, stand up and be counted
(don't you *want* to be a woman?). WOMEN—this
last and final women is our White House of femininity, the ideal woman. This is the woman that
men love, cherish, and protect, that they take home
to mother and buy only the best for. This third
WOMEN is the woman women wish they were. It
is also the one we suspect we aren't.

By a semantical sleight-of-hand and the constant
switching of decks under the table, women are never
quite sure when they are being average, normal,
ideal, or even desirable.

Gentlemen Prefer Doormats

It might be asked why we should not encourage
the masculine and feminine traditions, the Promethean and the Confucian, for the sake of variety.
One can favor diversity and variety in a culture, but
a diversity that stems from individual choice and

not from group-mandate. While as Erich Fromm says, "Social conditions can be created which will develop the positive side of the peculiarities of persons, sexes, and national groups," [1] it worries us a little as to who is going to decide what peculiarities of persons, sexes, and national groups are positive and to be preserved.

When we learn that Fromm finds the positive side of women in their patience, reliability, intensity of love and development of erotic charm, and the positive side of men in initiative, activity, and courage, it becomes difficult to see what is to prevent the resultant social conditions from tending in the direction of the mother-warrior pattern.

Assuming for the moment that women, while comprising more than half the population, do display some signs of belonging to a minority, it can be noted that women are past masters of the deference game. Deference attitudes are bits of behavior which, like circus posters, announce that their possessor is someone who can be trusted to keep her place. A woman who wears high heels, white gloves, and a listening expression does not awaken suspicion. The ideal woman exhibits maximum deference toward men—revealed in a cajoling tone, a coy visage, a charming unreasonableness, and a disinterest in worldly affairs. With a good portrayal of helplessness, a woman is in line for all the rewards the society has to offer.

John Dollard has pointed out various of these "accommodation attitudes" as they occur in a caste society of our day; his work is *Caste and Class in a Southern Town*.[2] He discovered a marked tendency among members of an underprivileged caste to find themselves a patron, an "angel," who would protect them from an otherwise hostile society.

Insofar as men and women fit into such a scheme, the angel or patron is found in the institution of the husband. By adopting the woman, he promises to protect her against a social regime that otherwise makes small provision for her protection. The trouble with a patronage system, however, is that kindness and gallantry operate only toward one's own protégé, one's wife and daughters in this case. The attitude of an angel toward outside suppliants (especially if not of the preferred age or façade, or if these observe different habits at table) becomes not only unprotective but predatory. The dictum of women and children first applies in our society only to women and children of one's own social group. This leaves unprotected a great many persons who have for one reason or another been unable to procure an angel of sufficient purchasing power.

When a member of a social group which depends on patronage begins to find life unsatisfactory, she will have special ways of meeting her problem. A minority group by definition lacks a sense of participation in the control of their society. They therefore turn to magic to solve their dilemmas. Magic does not attempt realistically to alter the course of events.

"Magic accept the *status quo*," writes Dollard; "it takes the place of political activity, agitation, organization, solidarity, or any real moves to change status." As we all know, magic works. The medicine man brings honest drops of rain, and the woman behind the hand cream really gets her man.

Through their neurotic fear of being abandoned,

women will go through meaningless rituals of self-reassurance, which occupy them autistically, blot out reality, and offer a sense of safety. "During their neurosis," writes Masserman, "many animals licked, cleaned, and preened themselves excessively, courted an unusual amount of fondling by the experimenter [the angel], and often reacted aggressively toward other animals." Cat 60, for example, "began to clean and lick herself almost continually; when the feeding signals were given she would merely glance at the food-box, vocalize plaintively, and then intensify her preening behavior."

Different cats reacted differently to their insecurities, as do people, as do women.* It was noted that "animals placed in emotionally conflictful situations sometimes react with exaggerated and often ludicrous playfulness." Some animals which had been meek and docile became aggressive and vicious. Cats frequently developed mannerisms. A typical symptom of growing insecurity was "marked startle responses to minor sensory stimuli"—the "sensitivity" of women.

And when it came to males subjected to the same conflictful situations, the result was similar. "Cat 14, a normally independent and self-sufficient animal, after three air-blasts became excessively timid, invariably tried to hide his head under the experimenter's arm while being handled, and would rub against the experimenter's legs or climb on his shoulder as an invitation to be fondled and petted." [3]

* "While cats, in our own experience and in that of almost all other workers, differ greatly in their individual capacities and characteristics, there is no indication in our own work and in most other reports that any of these differences are related to the sex of the animal."

Education in Deference

It is sometimes said that women do not
particularly profit from a college education, and it is
a waste of time to give it to them; that women
think by intuition rather than logic; that women do
not enjoy free sallies of the mind but prefer small
chores, routine preoccupations, and acts of faith.[4]

Education is discouraged for a group in whom a
free choice between alternatives is considered socially dangerous. If a society wishes to enforce a situation in which a minority is to be limited in its
choices and activities, it does its best to deny the
group an education. Education has a way of opening up new vistas of freedom and potentiality. If a
social minority decides to strive for better education, it will find it expedient to argue that better
schooling will make better and more deferential
members of the group. Education (the Negroes in
the Southern town argued) would make prompter,
tidier, more polite and useful servants for white
people.

The earliest feminists claimed that education
would make women better cooks, nurses, and com-
panions for their children. They dared not mention
the development of powers of thought, of self-
expression, or the pleasures of the free intellect.
And young ladies' vocational seminaries, or finishing
schools, were the first educational concession women
won.

Free education threatens the caste boundaries in
a society. Students discover that alternatives of action can be contemplated by a simple exercise of
the mind. Contemplating alternative modes of be-

havior may mean choosing a mode that goes against the grain of the caste system. Women are supposed to remain childlike and intuitive. If insights remain haphazard and are a vague feeling-things-out, the caste status feels safe.

"*But they turn against us the little education which unhappily they get hold of*, some husbands might say," wrote Stendhal. "No doubt; and Napoleon was also quite right not to give arms to the National Guard. . . . Arm a man and then continue to oppress him, and you will see that he can be so perverse as to turn his arms against you as soon as he can."

Society is charmed by the irrationality of women. It approves of their extravagance and folly. Advertising[5] plays upon the insecurity of the female who, unable actively to confront her problems, is eager to swallow any panacea on the market. Women at beauty shops, women before their mirrors, women gossiping (effigy-burning), women giggling, weeping, coquetting are women who do not threaten social change. "A man likes to be able to say of his slave: *She's too big a fool to be a knave*"—again Stendhal.

That minority group which most cheerfully adopts its deference role is best liked and most kindly thought of. While one which does not accept the prejudgment of its inferiority (or peculiar limitations) but moves ahead to competitive achievements is hugely resented. Today women cannot decide whether to be abnormal and achieve something, or be normal and abandon their ambitions.

Women, to borrow a phrase of Mistress Overdone, are weary of being custom-shrunk.

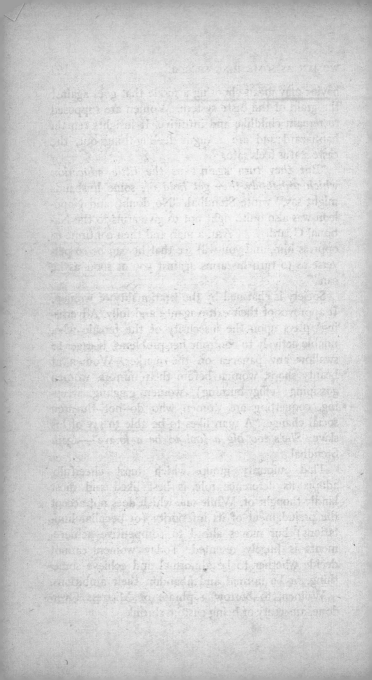

CHAPTER FIFTEEN

a world of differences

Man is a rational animal, but only women can have babies.

UNKNOWN

The history of mankind has been the search for some difference between individuals and groups of individuals—color, geographical location, sex—that would really count for something, a difference on the basis of which society could get organized, once and for all, and settle down to a peaceful senility. For some reason, the mere discovery of such a difference has meant that one group of people became subordinated to another group. And sooner or later the subordinate group would kick up a fuss.

The marked difference that distinguishes women from men is one of the most palpable differences to be found. It is women who have babies, men who cannot. Among legislative groups, in fact, women are sometimes regarded simply as the pregnant species. While only women can have babies, it must be remembered that they are not always having them. Women, during the childbearing period between adolescence and menopause, are not even fertile much of the time.

Dr. Dickinson has expressed it in this way, "The target, the ovum, is exposed only one-sixtieth of the time, a total of some seven whole days in the entire

year, or a half-day thirteen times in that span. . . .
As it is, Hartman declares that the difficulties in the
way of conception are such that the human female
should be classed actually as of low fertility." [1]

Fertility is not a fixed condition in women, nor
should it invariably be taken advantage of. The
need for spacing children is recognized today, and
consideration of the health of the mother is granted
to be of some importance. Whether a given pregnancy will add a new life or transform existing children into orphans is no idle query. One-fourth of
the maternal deaths in the United States occur un-
necessarily, because the mothers are victims of
chronic disease processes which make it impossible
for them to survive pregnancy. [2] Strangely enough, it
is the over-idealization of the maternal instinct
which accounts for thousands of neglected children
among us.

How Much Is Instinct?

Science has sought to test in lower animals what
it unromantically terms the maternal *drive*. A
mother rat, it was found, will heroically cross an un-
pleasantly charged grill, receiving an electric shock,
in order to rescue her helpless young on the other
side. But how long does her heroism persist? As E.
C. Tolman, the psychologist, reports: "It varies in a
predictable way with the age of the young, the state
of the mammillary glands, and the like." [3] When the
young animals grow a bit older, the mother will no
longer cross the electric grill to rescue her own flesh
and blood, not even her favorite son that inherited
its father's bead eyes.

The maternal instinct in humans is not predicated on the condition of the mammillary glands. The maternal instinct is a great and stimulating ideal because it comprises traits not so specifically maternal as human. The qualities we attribute to motherhood are basically human qualities; they include a warm regard for other persons, their needs and difficulties. That this entire complex of sympathy should today be subsumed under the maternal instinct, thus making "love" a female responsibility, helps account for the state of the world. The better factors afloat in maternalism—considerateness, generosity, protectiveness—are scarcely the temperamental monopoly of the female. Nor can women be called upon to establish international peace simply by exerting mother love in all directions; not while they continue to bring up their male children in a tradition that regards concern for other people's needs as unmanly.

The maternal instinct in women is frequently illustrated by an image of a tigress who defends her young against all threats, fiercely and, we like to think, successfully. We find equally prevalent a picture of motherhood typified by utter, or even abject, helplessness. As Havelock Ellis describes it, "In woman, the long period of pregnancy and lactation, and the prolonged helplessness of her child, render her for a considerable period of her life economically dependent." [4]

Yet the tigress is not notably dependent during the prolonged helplessness of her young, and neither—come to think of it—is primitive or modern woman, who usually goes right on with her heavy housework a few weeks after childbirth. In fact,

housework is often increased by the birth of a child.
It is true that the woman has a protector, and that
he goes off to the office every day where he sits quietly at a desk earning money. But the helpless
young mother may be at home doing a washing that
requires three times the muscular exertion he ex-
pends.

With the image of the protective tigress we satisfy
ourselves that mother love is a sufficient antidote for
poverty, chronic ill-health, or any injustice; while
with the helplessness of motherhood we enjoy the
thought that a woman is throughout life dependent
on man's good will and protection.

How Different Are Differences?

That women can have babies and men cannot is
a genuine difference between the sexes. Does this
mean that the similarities between women are
greater than their differences, and that these similarities are more important than any similarities they
share with men? "Regardless of the social differences between women in different cultures or classes,
from the primitive to the most civilized, and the
most sophisticated to the most lowly," writes
Amram Scheinfeld, "they share many vital experiences—the menstrual process, motherhood and
their relationships to men—which bring them together in their thoughts, personality, and behavior." [5]

The mere mention of vital experiences, as esoteri-
cally possessed by women, has heretofore silenced
any tendency on the part of women to question the
uniformity of those overwhelming determiners of
character, menstruation and childbirth. To speak of

vital experiences is like talking about love. No one really believes that love is the same for every individual, but the generalization is pleasant.

This stress on the joyous uniformity of women's subjective experiences has been made for the most part by men, who express at the same time their jealous inability to participate in these purely feminine experiences. It is the male author who so often tells us in detail why certain physiological processes, such as menstruation, are exercising a conclusive influence on our thoughts, personality, and behavior. Yet, speaking from their own premises, who is less qualified to judge these vital experiences than the sex which admits it has been excluded from them?

If women were asked what they actually thought about these shared experiences—whether they found them exciting, terrifying, tedious, expected or unexpected—society would be disillusioned by the diversity of the answers. Do women's "relationships to men" really bring them closer together than their interest in different men marks them apart? *What on earth can she see in him!*

On Being Ourselves

It seemed to Aristotle that man, as the one rational animal, ought to stick to rationalizing. When man was not reasoning, he became mere animal, vegetable, or mineral. Thanks to an enlarged forebrain, it was discovered that man of all beasts was able to set up abstract standards of behavior uniquely capable of embarrassing those who did not live up to them. Thus man came to distinguish himself as the animal-with-symbols, the idealist and the standard-bearer, as well as the most embarrassed.

In this development of the creative differences of man, as distinct from other fauna, two capabilities have been overlooked, at least by philosophers. One of these is the erect carriage; man is the only primate who makes even a sporting attempt to stand up straight. Secondly, man is the only mammal with a thumb opposite to his fingers.

When we look about us, we find that the aristocratic tradition has indeed cultivated the erect carriage as the outstanding feature of man, leaning backward ever so slightly in order to show a clear advance over the gibbons. Industrialists, on the other hand, have developed the assembly line expressly to provide an outlet for man's unique ability for grasping, nailing, hammering, and other digital triumphs.

Perhaps it is these vital pinching-experiences which bring all men together in their thoughts, personality, and behavior. The chimpanzee may have a thumb, but it is not opposite to the fingers. He can swing aimlessly from tree to tree, but is never found settling down on the installment plan. For this requires a pinching aptitude he does not possess, one only dimly foreshadowed in squirrels and other of the more prudent rodents.

From time to time man has gone mad with pride over his uniquenesses, especially his difference from women and his difference from the other animals. In truth there is something stirring about man's upright carriage. His infinite patience with pinching together bits of machinery and small change is also noteworthy. Man's power of abstract thought is unexampled: his ability to subtract one reality from another and come out with something like the *Ding-an-sich* that smells and tastes realer than the original ingredients.

Yet there is no rule by which we must develop only what we have "uniquely" to offer (like a freak in the circus); we should be allowed an expression of choice as to which of our multiple capabilities we wish to exert. The progressive school with its admonition to "be creative" often has preconceptions of what the creative is to be. These premeditated potentialities are given a few years of grace in which to emerge, but if they have not come out of hiding by that time—back to the birch rod.

While women's ability to bear children is one of the most unique and impressive to be found, women are also rational animals with a pinching dexterity, an erect carriage, and certain other qualities. Must a woman cultivate only that uniqueness which distinguishes her from man (and links her with the animals), or is she to be allowed to exhibit some purely human characteristics as well?

If the human animal chooses on occasion to become a runner of marathons, we need not protest that he is bringing down on us the ridicule of all odd-toed ungulates, who also possess a faculty for running and a better one. Man may want to indulge his kinship with the animals at times, thus distinguishing himself from the motionless tomato and from the minerals who possess such alarming permanence. Human society would in any case be more pleasant to live with if man remembered more often that he is the only laughing animal.

CHAPTER SIXTEEN

here are the facts

There is a tide in the affairs of men,
Which taken at the flood, leads on to fortune:
Omitted, all the voyage of their life,
Is bound in shallows, and in miseries.

BRUTUS, in *Julius Caesar*

It is estimated that eight out of every ten human pregnancies succeed; two out of ten will terminate abnormally. The guinea pig, who propagates so lavishly, loses fewer of its young during gestation than the human female; though one might suppose women had at their command all the resources of modern science. The truth of it is, modern science shows a certain reticence toward lifting the veil around feminine mysteries, even one of the more callous mysteries such as the high ratio of structural abnormality among the human young.

Women accept the risks of pregnancy with extraordinary patience, and a miscarriage during the first month, the second, the third; the death of a child born prematurely; the birth of an imperfect child—these are regarded in a fatalistic light, as something science would surely do something about if it possibly could.

The sad fact is that one of the most significant discoveries in this connection has been gathering moss for eight years while science devoted itself to the more interesting feat of splitting the atom. The reducing of abnormal pregnancies in women may require the accurate discovery of time of ovulation, perhaps even that hour at which an egg is newly released from the ovary. This prospect causes society some apprehension.

How could science prove when its predictions had been correct as to time of ovulation? A direct proof is by examination of the ovaries; an indirect proof is when conception occurs at the time predicted.

Two clues to the cycle are the fluctuations of basal body temperature each month and the related fluctuations in the cellular content of the vaginal mucosa. For example, around the time of ovulation there is a sharp drop in body temperature, reaching a low* for the month, followed by a rapid rise. This requires a day or two at the most. By direct examination of the ovaries during abdominal operations, it has been demonstrated that science is not only capable of estimating the general period of ovulation but of stating with considerable certainty that the egg will be released shortly after the rise in temperature begins.[1]

In other words, while laymen are inclined to believe that ovulation in women is so erratic a thing that science has no hope of catching up with it, specialists in the field take it for granted that they can predict the general location of ovulation in individual women at a particular time; they are busy trying to predict the span of *hours* during which the egg is released.

* Perhaps "heat" will be found to correlate with "the period of lowest temperature"—an oxymoron of the first order.

Time Is of the Essence

Some years ago an experiment was conducted that should have transformed the face of the earth or at least reached the daily newspapers. It did not. Two scientists, Dr. Richard J. Blandau and Dr. William C. Young, published a paper on "The Effects of Delayed Fertilization on the Development of the Guinea Pig Ovum." [2] The upshot was that if an egg newly released from the ovary was not fertilized *at once*, it became an increasingly unworthy transmitter of new life.

Over half the miscarriages in women are today referred vaguely to a germ plasm deficiency.[3] Scientists admit that this phrase is a catch-all for miscarriages they do not understand. It suggests an early inadequacy in the embryo* which interferes with implantation and growth, rather than an accident which befalls the embryo several weeks after pregnancy has begun. Might women's high rate of miscarriage—two for every eight normal births—be attributable in any degree to the utilization of eggs which have waited too long in the fallopian tubes after release from the ovary?

Heat in animals, we incline to think, occurs at the moment of the release of the egg, thus encouraging fertilization by the male. Actually heat precedes

* Certain words in this connection are used interchangeably. The united sperm and egg are "the zygote." More frequently in embryology this is called "the ovum," although ovum at other times means the *un*fertilized egg. "Ovum" (or plural, "ova") refers to the earliest stage of development, and contains the embryo. Since pathological embryos, as found in miscarriages, are often greatly retarded in development, they are likely to be termed pathological ova.

ovulation in animals. In the guinea pig, heat (or the
time at which the female's interest in the male
reaches an observable intensity) commences ten
hours *before* ovulation. Ten hours later heat has
ceased. The female peremptorily refuses copulation
although she may still possess unfertilized ova. Why
is this? After ovulation occurs, she does not permit
advances by the male.

Thus heat in the lower animals must be thought
of not only as a period during which fertilization is
encouraged, but as a period to which fertilization is
peculiarly *limited*.

That the human female does not have a sharply
defined period of heat, thus encouraging fertilization, has not seemed of importance for her health or
well-being. But the fact that she lacks a period to
which fertilization is *limited* may prove of major importance—both for her own health and for the
health of her young.

In order to test the effect of age on the guinea pig
ovum (age as computed in hours), it was necessary
to artificially introduce spermatozoa into the female
tract. These test guinea pigs were sexually unwilling,
therefore; and would ordinarily have refused insemination.* The pregnancies that resulted from the fertilization of "aging" ova were then studied, and
were found to reveal an increasing number of abnormalities and structural malformations as the age
at which the egg had been fertilized increased.

In the horse, the cow, the ewe, the sow and the
guinea pig, the release of the egg occurs toward the

* Insemination means introducing-of-sperm, whether pregnancy
results or not. Fertilization or impregnation indicates the successful union of sperm and egg.

end of heat or shortly after. In the cat and the rabbit ovulation occurs only after the stimulus of copulation. "Thus in several mammals, at least," write Blandau and Young, "the reproductive processes are so timed that spermatozoa are in the fallopian tubes and ready to enter the egg immediately after it has been extruded from the follicle." *

In the human female ovulation occurs regularly and spontaneously, in response to fluctuations of the cycle; this is akin to the horse, the ewe, and the guinea pig. It does not occur in response to the stimulus of copulation. If it is important for the sperm to enter the egg immediately after it has been expelled from the ovary, it is clear that the human female has at present no safeguard which would insure fertilization of a new egg, freshly released. This safeguard could be provided if the accurate determination of time of ovulation were available.[4]

The experiment with the guinea pigs demonstrated that when an egg was eight hours old, the risk of an abnormal pregnancy was almost 200 percent greater than the risk run by an egg fertilized at the proper time. Eight hours is not an especially long time, but it apparently was long enough. Some eggs were experimentally fertilized after they had remained fourteen hours in the fallopian tube. Their risk of abnormal pregnancy became six times the risk of an egg freshly fertilized.[5]

Not only was the risk of abnormalities greater in the experimental group, but the possibility of sterility was increased. This latter fact had been known for some time in connection with the breeding of

* It looks as though the patient receptive egg might give way to the patiently waiting sperm.

domestic animals: that an ovum does not remain
viable or fertile very long, and if fertilization is
delayed after ovulation, the litter will be reduced. In
the human female where there is only one ovum
present at a time, delayed fertilization would even
more seriously reduce chances of pregnancy. For
women suffering from functional sterility, therefore,
knowledge of exact time of ovulation is important,
and this knowledge is widely employed in this connection.[6]

Concerning the role played by an "aging" sperm,
experiment has shown that the sperm, unlike the
egg, does not slowly and gradually deteriorate; it ex-
pires suddenly.[7] Spermatozoa were experimentally
introduced some hours *before* the commencement
of heat. By the time the female ovulated, therefore,
the sperm were nearing their age-limit. It was found
that in these cases there was less chance of impregnation occurring. On the other hand, when pregnancies did result, they were not marked by the high incidence of abnormality that occurred when an aging
egg was used.

Perhaps the patriarchal biologist will want to add
this interesting detail to his account, on the ground
that the sperm dies a hero's death, suddenly and at
the peak of his powers. The matriarchal biologist
will doubtless counter by claiming the sperm is giving up too easily, while the female ovum fights off
the tug of death till all hope is abandoned.

We have no way of knowing how often among
women an ovum that is eight, fourteen, or twenty
hours old is fertilized and pregnancy begun. It is interesting, however, that the ratio of miscarriage in

women should approximate that of the artificially fertilized guinea pigs, in which aging eggs have been utilized.

Guinea pigs that were impregnated only fourteen hours after ovulation failed in seven out of ten cases to complete the pregnancy. Guinea pigs fertilized twenty hours after release of the egg (only one day late) had nine abnormal pregnancies for every normal one.

The structural malformations and abnormalities in the embryos lost by these animals are the same type of imperfections found in human embryos. Dr. Franklin P. Mall summarized the pattern of human pregnancies in this way: "Eighty out of 100 pregnancies end in the birth of normal individuals; seven are aborted as pathological ova containing radical changes within them; and about one (.06) produces a monster at term. The remaining twelve 'normal' fetuses and embryos are by no means all normal, for we are constantly finding in them, especially the younger specimens, minor changes which must be viewed as forerunners to real monsters." [8]

We cannot regret the miscarriage of embryos imperfectly formed, but we should bend every effort to reducing their occurrence. While delayed fertilization may be only one factor in the picture, it deserves further research and application to humans. To apply the results of an experiment on guinea pigs to human beings may seem a far leap in species, but the leap is no greater than from guinea pig to chimpanzee. Dr. Yerkes recommends that delayed fertilization be avoided in the breeding of chimpanzees.

The Evolution of Monster-Forms

The rate of growth during the first weeks of life is extremely rapid. The child—or embryo—passes swiftly through one phase after another, assuming many different forms as the various tissues develop and the organs become established. Not for some time does the embryo begin to assume a characteristically human shape. And not until the seventh month is the child considered viable, which means that if born at this time, it yet has a chance at life.

During these rapid changes, the young embryo's struggle for existence goes on: the ovum must become imbedded in the uterus, the placenta must form, and a constant supply of nourishment be provided. After the fourth month, growth is primarily in size, but during the first weeks when the embryo is striving toward a certain *form*, rate of growth and balance of growth are as important as amount of growth. Different tissues must develop at different crucial periods in the prenatal life, and an interference with growth at one time will produce one type of abnormality while interference at another stage of growth causes distortions of another sort.*

This explains the evolution of different varieties of abnormality, and it is clear that the process which produces them is perfectly natural once the ovum is off to a bad start. Since vital organs like the placenta (through which nourishment is passed from

* The heart and brain develop very early; interruption in this phase of growth produces one group of "monsters." Later, the heart and brain prove resistant, but then it is time for the head and the extremities to grow. If this stage of growth is retarded, distortions of these portions occur.

mother to child) and the heart and central nervous system begin to form very early, any momentary pause in development is likely to cause malformation, death, and miscarriage.[9] If a pathological embryo survives the second month, it will probably continue through pregnancy and the mother will give birth to a child with some clearly recognized malformation.*

Monsters, and pathological embryos termed "young monsters," are *not* hereditary forms, are never hereditary forms. When Mall wrote his *Pathology of the Human Ovum* in 1910, he did not even deign to include hereditary malformations such as polydactyly and muscle anomalies. These form part of his *normal* group of eighty out of each hundred pregnancies. The twenty *failures* of pregnancy result from the influence of adverse environmental conditions on normal ova. Since monster-forms are produced by an interference with growth, or the failure to become properly implanted, Mall suspected that a number of the abnormalities were being caused by a diseased condition in the uterus. Later he rejected inflammation of the uterus as a sole or necessary cause.

One can imagine how women may have reacted in the course of history to these various emendations of medical theory. First, monster-forms were believed to be hereditary; happily this was dis-

---

* If an alteration in the young embryo is *very slight*, it may allow the infant to survive. However, even an alteration that is slight in the embryo, or ovum, will present a well-recognized malformation at birth, after seven or eight months of growth. Hare-lip and clubfoot are minor anomalies of this sort. There is no need therefore to fear "hidden" imperfections resulting from pathological ova.

proved. Next a diseased condition in the uterus
was held responsible—a conclusion which must
have awakened a certain remorse in women, feeling
it was an inadequacy in their system that doomed
the child. Today among women miscarriage is usually attributed to excessive physical exertion. While
exertion may be an accompanying factor, it is not
considered by medical men to be the primary cause.

Perhaps it is believed that women will be discouraged by something termed germ plasm deficiency—
particularly when no means of prevention has yet
been discovered. Yet germ plasm deficiency does
not return us to a hereditary source of abnormal
pregnancy. In fact, if the delayed fertilization
hypothesis is true for humans, a unique reconcilia-
tion of the *germinal* and *environmental* explana-
tions can take place, as well as an excellent possibility for prevention.

Heredity or Environment

Mall had several strong arguments against the germinal school of thought, which believed some fault
in the original germ cells was causing faulty implantation, disorganization, and miscarriage. He pointed
out that the same types of abnormal embryos were
being produced experimentally in fish, frogs, and
chickens simply by subjecting the fertilized egg to
adverse environmental conditions.

When such eggs were treated with various salts, or
in some cases shaken, or their temperature radically
altered, malformations of the embryo would occur,
similar to those in humans.[10] It seemed clear that an
adverse environment produced monsters. The envi-

ronment of the human embryo, being the uterus it-self, was therefore suspect. And since inflammations of the uterus often accompanied miscarriage, most gynecologists at that time believed a diseased condition was here interfering with proper implantation, or even poisoning the embryo—a view no longer held.

Mall's second argument against the germinal theory was this: *if* the cause of pathology lies in the original germ cells rather than in an adverse environment, the ova found in tubal pregnancies should contain the same percentage of structural malformation as ova recovered from uterine pregnancies. But ova found in the tubes show an overwhelming incidence of gross pathologies—as high as 96 per cent. Again Mall pointed to environment as the cause of this, for in the unnatural surroundings of the fallopian tube the ovum could not possibly become properly implanted.

Pathologies of the ovum remain among the major human mysteries. "Few subjects," writes Dr. Nicholas J. Eastman in a recent book, *Progress in Gynecology,* "rest upon such an uncertain and unsatisfactory basis as does the etiology of habitual abortion. Obviously, there can be only two main causes, defective germ cells and faulty maternal environment." * [11] The classic debate between germinal fac-

---

* In medical literature miscarriage is generally referred to as spontaneous abortion, distinct from induced. "Habitual abortion" is commonly used to indicate two or more miscarriages *in succession.* Eastman believes this term should be reserved for cases in which spontaneous abortion occurs at least three times in succession. The reason behind this is the spontaneous cure rate. In habitual abortion there is relatively more possibility of maternal factors operating.

tors and environmental factors remains. Since Mall's time some causes have been eliminated from the lists and others have been postulated. While authorities are in agreement that defective germ plasm is the leading cause, it is the maternal "environmental" factors that we hear most about.

This is because the maternal factors, while explaining only a minority of miscarriages, are at least more easily observable, describable, and accessible to treatment. Uterine misplacement, hypertensive vascular disease, and syphilis are known causes. They are conditions preferably discovered before conception rather than after. However, uterine displacement can explain only a few of all miscarriages. Syphilis does not cause miscarriage before the fourth month, and can be treated. Hypertensive vascular disease is a cause of late not early abortion.

It is the miscarriages of early pregnancy that remain the most mysterious—and are most frequent. It is in these early weeks that most pathological embryos begin—and cannot be treated. "The largest number of pathological embryos are formed during the first seven weeks of pregnancy," writes Mall; "their number falls off markedly in the eighth and ninth weeks; and but very few occur after the tenth week."

What Caused the Cause?

It is all very well to trace the cause of abnormal pregnancy to germ plasm deficiency or faulty implantation, but most of us prefer causes which lead to treatment and prevention. Is there no hope of avoiding these abnormalities? A rather indirect hope lies in what Eastman calls the spontaneous cure rate. One miscarriage does *not* tend to lead to another. Habitual abortion is less frequent than might be expected.

Consider a representative group of well over 1000 women: ten percent will prove sterile. We will assume that 1000 achieve a first pregnancy. Suppose 900 of these women have successful pregnancies and 100 abort.* If these 100 women attempt a second pregnancy, according to the spontaneous cure rate only about thirteen will abort a second time. And if the thirteen women who have miscarried twice in succession attempt a third pregnancy, only five will miscarry and eight will succeed.

Only when a woman has miscarried three times in succession does Eastman term it habitual abortion; for here the chances of a fourth miscarriage become substantially greater. Of the five remaining women, only one will have a fair chance of not aborting the fourth time.†

On the whole this picture is an optimistic one, since of 1000 women, all but four have succeeded in achieving a normal pregnancy. In our enthusiasm over this spontaneous cure rate, we should not overlook the fact that 122 miscarriages have taken place along the way—or more if the four women continue to conceive. The word *cure* is something of a misnomer, in fact, since it is not so much that one miscarriage is "cured" as that a second or third is somehow being prevented.

---

* Mall gives 20 percent as *total* lost; Eastman, 10 percent.[13]
† Thus for women who have aborted once, the spontaneous cure rate is 86.8 percent. For women who have aborted twice in succession, the spontaneous cure rate is 63.1 percent. For women who have had three consecutive abortions, the spontaneous cure rate drops to 16.4 percent.

Miscarriage affords no particular benefit to a woman's health,[13] and since it also indicates a deeper-lying fault in the ovum, preferably avoided, it might be worthwhile to speculate about some of the things a delayed fertilization hypothesis might say about the facts and theses so far advanced.

The Hazards of Youth

The pregnancy of the guinea pig lasts about seventy days. If we divide this into a first phase, second phase and third phase and consider the group of guinea pigs artificially fertilized after ovulation, we find Blandau and Young attributing *most* pregnancy failures of the first phase to delayed fertilization, *probably some* failures of the second phase to the same cause, but none of the failures of the third phase to the fact that an aging egg was used. After the fifty-fifth day, that is, the losses in the artificially fertilized group of guinea pigs were no greater than the losses in the normally fertilized group, and therefore these late-pregnancy accidents must be attributed to other factors.[14]

On analogy then, one might expect delayed fertilization to have nothing whatever to do with miscarriages occurring during the last three months of human pregnancy: this is the time when "miscarriage" begins to be called "stillbirth" or "premature labor." Nor would one expect delayed fertilization to be the major cause of miscarriages during the second three months of pregnancy, though possibly of some.

All that remains is the initial phase of human pregnancy, the first twelve weeks. Here delayed fer-

tilization may play a major role in success or failure;
and it is within this short span of time that over
eighty percent of human miscarriages do occur. Also
within this short span most of the serious pathologies develop. It is here that germ plasm deficiency
has been settled on as the leading cause of abnormality.

Any factor interfering with or retarding the
normal rate of growth is likely to produce
malformations. Malformations have been produced
in fish and frog embryos by mechanical and chemical interference with the environment of the egg.
*The same type of malformation has been produced
in fish and frog embryos by subjecting the original
egg-cell to delayed fertilization.*[15]

Mall pointed to the monster-forms artificially produced in fish and frogs as proof of an environmental
cause of pathologies. The delayed fertilization hypothesis could point to recent experiments, which
produced monster-forms in fish and frogs by use of
aging eggs, as proof that late fertilization is the
prime culprit in pathological ova. Which of these
factors is the human embryo more likely to be exposed to?

It is easy to tamper with the detached eggs of fish
and frogs, shaking them, treating them with salt,
and so on; but the human mother affords a unique
protection against such interruptions of growth.
Violent shaking sometimes occurs, but this is certainly an infrequent cause of miscarriage. The
human infant is further guarded against the abrupt
temperature changes that have such an adverse effect
on proper growth in fish and frogs. As to protection
against chemical shock, the mother in her own re-

fusal of adverse chemicals indirectly protects the child. The placenta also helps "filter" from the mother's blood only that nourishment which the child needs. The child can draw on the mother's own supply of calcium. It gives up its waste products into her blood.

Thus the human infant, being a mammal, is remarkably well protected against some of the dangers that confront the eggs of fish and frogs. But there is one factor that *Homo sapiens* is least protected against, and that is the possibility of delayed fertilization. Because heat in humans is either non-existent or non-operative, ova are undoubtedly fertilized quite frequently after prolonged delay.

What is suggested by "germ plasm deficiency"? Germ plasm can refer either to sperm or egg. Both sperm and egg bear genes, one the paternal hereditary genes, the other the maternal. But hereditary factors do not cause monsters. What then is one primary difference between egg and sperm?

The egg is larger than the sperm because it has in it the food supply for the prospective embryo. The embryo is, at first, entirely dependent on this food reserve for its growth. Since the age of the sperm does not affect the embryo's survival or normality as the age of the egg does, we can wonder if it is the *food reserve* in the egg that is deteriorating. This food reserve influences the early growth of the embryo.

On the way to the uterus the tiny fertilized ovum must undergo segmentation or division and become a solid mass of rounded cells. The larger inner cells form the embryo. The outer cells help absorb nutriment from the lining of the uterus. The ovum leads

an active life in its first weeks; it must work toward
a placental connection with the mother in order to
draw on her supply of nourishment by the time that
its own gives out. If pathologies are caused by retar-
dation in growth, one would expect any interruption in food supply to produce overwhelming fatalities.

For Mall, the cause of pathological ova was
"faulty implantation": "on account of faulty implantation of the chorion [the membrane envel-
oping the embryo] the nutrition of the embryo is
affected, so that, if the ovum is very young the entire embryo is soon destroyed . . ." [16] Today the
main cause of pathological ova is still traced to
"faulty implantation," but the basic cause is believed to be "germ plasm deficiency," not an adverse
maternal environment.

The delayed fertilization hypothesis can effect a
wedding of the germinal and environmental expla-
nations of pathological ova. For according to it the
fault would lie in a deficiency in the germ plasm,
but a deficiency caused by adverse environment—a
period of delay. If it is the food reserve in the egg
that deteriorates, the basic cause would lie in the
very "environment" of the embryo—that is, in the
ovum that surrounds it.

An embryo, endowed with superior hereditary
genes, might have the best intentions in the world
of assuming a normal human shape; but if its food
supply fails it, it has no chance whatever of maintaining a normal rate of growth. No wonder death
so often occurs at the very time that the placenta
should be forming.

If delayed fertilization occurs in humans, it will

occur on a basis of chance. The chances are against
dice falling the same way twice, and the laws of
probability make it unlikely that delayed fertilization would occur again and again in the same
woman. What best reduces this chance is that the
fertility of the egg tends to decrease at the same
time that its vitality is lowered. Otherwise we would
expect an even higher ratio of abnormality. Perhaps
it will be found that some ova are predisposed to
deteriorate more slowly, thus to live longer; this
would accordingly raise the chance of late fertilization.

Delayed fertilization would thus be an "accidental" factor rather than a "recurrent" one.* It is some
mysterious accidental factor that is operating
through the spontaneous cure rate, producing miscarriage at one time and not at another, dooming
one pregnancy and allowing a second to terminate
successfully. While these companion facts do not
prove the delayed fertilization hypothesis, they give
it support. Delayed fertilization would reveal itself
in the same spirit of chance that miscarriage and the
spontaneous cure rate already reveal.

When Mall found a much higher ratio of gross abnormalities in tubal pregnancies, one wonders if he
was finding a higher ratio of late-fertilized ova. No
one understands why an ovum should on occasion
wish to remain in the fallopian tube rather than
continue its journey to the uterus. If aging ova have
lowered vitality, it is not impossible that they are
more lethargic in carrying out their duties, some-

---

* Ten percent of all pregnancies will terminate in spontaneous abortion, 9.6 percent from accidental causes and 0.4 percent from recurrent factors.[17]

times remaining in the tubes and contributing to the high ratio of abnormality found there.

The Difficult First Day of Life

The vocabulary changes somewhat in a discussion of late-pregnancy hazards, but the basic principle remains: any arrest in growth or nutrition endangers the child. This is important not alone for normality but for survival itself. Until one reaches the 70- and 80-year age groups, one does not find so high a death rate as that which exists in this country among children under one year of age. Even when these deaths can be attributed to unfavorable prenatal conditions, they are seldom regarded as reproductive accidents, as failures of pregnancy which they are.

Cancer research has received great impetus because we know that one out of eight will die unless a cure or prevention is discovered. Yet how many know that one child out of every five is lost even before pregnancy is completed? How many know that two out of every five children born prematurely die, and that 90,000 premature births occur annually? [18] that 11,038 children died before the age of one, in 1940, due to congenital malformations; while still others lived, crippled and handicapped? [19]

The embryologist sees things from his own particular perspective, from the point of view of his interest in the earliest phases of pregnancy. Thus Mall was inclined to regard any child that survived to term as *normal*. One out of five pregnancies, he wrote, would terminate abnormally in spontaneous abortion or—rarely—in the birth of a monster. The

remaining four pregnancies would "end in the birth
of a normal individual." But is a stillborn child a
normal individual? Is a child born with a clubfoot or
a harelip to be accounted normal? Is a premature
birth normal, when two-fifths of such children do
not survive?

Yerkes makes a similar error when he compares
the frequency of reproductive accidents among laboratory chimpanzees with the frequency of such accidents among humans. Among chimpanzees the ratio
of accidents is surprisingly high, he writes, there
being one accident to every two normal births.
"This may be contrasted with the human ratio,
which, according to different authorities, ranges
from 1:2.5 to 1:5." * [20]

In the human ratios quoted, however, "accidents"
include only spontaneous abortions or miscarriages.
In the chimpanzee ratio, Yerkes has included stillbirths and non-surviving premature births among reproductive accidents. The human ratio is made
more optimistic than it actually is, for non-surviving
premature births and stillbirths are being added to
the "credit" side of the ledger.

As in the chimpanzee ratio, these losses should be
subtracted from the credit side and added to the
debit side, that is, to the reproductive accidents
among humans. Only when a candid and comprehensive view is taken of human reproduction, its
successes and its problems, will research be increased and remedies be sought, as in the case of
cancer, infantile paralysis, and other public con-
cerns.

* That is, one accident to two-and-one-half normal births; or
in the second case, one to five. Mall's estimate is one to four.

Fully 73,000 stillbirths occur annually in the United States. Thirty-six thousand non-surviving premature births occur. Adding these to the 11,038 deaths resulting from congenital malformations, we find 120,038 infant deaths directly attributable to accidents of pregnancy; they are losses which originate in unfavorable prenatal conditions. Some, or even most, of the cases of congenital malformation may be traceable to delayed fertilization, which could be prevented. Other adverse factors are nutritional and environmental, both amenable to correction. "Experience in our [chimpanzee] colony," writes Yerkes, "shows that the risk of other kinds of reproductive accident than early abortion is relatively slight, if climatic and nutritional conditions are held favorable and the pregnant female is provided with suitable social environment and protected from aggression." [21]

A recent study has shown the direct influence of nutrition on reducing late-pregnancy hazards. In a group of women whose diet was poor, stillbirth occurred in 3.4 percent of the cases. Another group of women with similarly poor diets were experimentally provided with supplemental foods during pregnancy; no stillbirths occurred among them. In the first group with poor diets, premature births occurred in 8 percent of the cases; among the group given supplemental foods, only 2.2 percent of the deliveries were premature.[22]

Nutrition is not the only factor in stillbirth and premature birth,* but it is an important one. It is

* Syphilis and the toxemias of pregnancy also cause stillbirth and premature birth. Toxemias are especially pernicious when pregnancy is repeated before an earlier toxemia has disap-

the indirect cause of still other deaths. By far the
chief cause of mortality in infants under one year is
premature birth, which we have discussed in relation to nutrition. The second highest cause is influ-
enza and pneumonia, clearly related to the amount
of resistance the child brings with it. In 1940 this
cause alone claimed 17,577 lives. The third highest
cause is congenital malformation, the result of arrested growth. The fourth highest cause is injury at
birth, accounting for 10,506 deaths in 1940; while
this is not dependent on nutrition, its incidence
could be reduced.

To include these tragedies among "normal births"
and then transfer them a few days or months later
to "infant mortality tables" may be more reassuring
to us, but it causes their loss to be ignored. "Maternal deaths, infant deaths and illness . . . are directly
associated with poverty, congested living, and lack
of even the minimum requirements for decent living
and adequate functioning"—came the report of the
National Resources Planning Board, which soon
found itself transferred to the mortality tables.

The Sixty-Four Dollar Question

The delayed fertilization hypothesis is not being
tested because it is felt the ovulatory cycle in
women is too indefinite and unpredictable. Delayed
fertilization cannot be avoided if the time of ovulation is not determined.

There are really three questions here perhaps:

---

peared. Hypertensive toxemias are the second most common
cause of maternal death. One hundred and fifty thousand
women suffer in some degree from these each year in the
United States.[23]

whether it would be *useful* to know the ovulatory
cycle in women, whether it would be *possible* to
know it, and whether it is *permissible* to know it.
Even if the first two questions are answered in the
affirmative, it is difficult to know what to say about
the third. The apple was eaten by Eve, and some
feel the wisest course is to keep knowledge out of
her reach henceforward. Yet the only index to
woman's freedom lies in her freedom to share in
those decisions which most profoundly affect her.
So far motherhood has not been considered one of
these areas.

Knowledge of the individual ovulatory cycle
would not only be useful in proving or disproving
the delayed fertilization hypothesis; it is important
in any diagnosis of abnormal ovarian conditions.
Therapy is governed by just these findings. To improve the chance of successful reproduction, the
ovulatory cycle in the laboratory chimpanzee is
studied for at least two or three months before pregnancy. "Irregularities of rhythm," writes Yerkes,
"may indicate either undesirable physiological characteristics or unfavorable environmental conditions,
whereas regularity and typicalness indicate the probability of normal reproductive process." [24]

In the case of the lower primates the cycle is more
readily determined, since it is visible and accompanied by heat. While in women the workings of the
cycle are more subtle and complex, methods exist by
which the individual rhythm can be studied. The
very "complications" which interfere with accurate
prediction are themselves suggestive of factors it
would be valuable to know about. A study pre-
dicting day of ovulation was described earlier, in

which direct examination of the ovaries was possible; of the few women who ran contrary to expectation, several had already displayed some type of atypical temperature-pattern, while two were found to have cysts.

If science achieves a mild degree of accuracy-of-prediction in a subject that interests it, its industry and enthusiasm know no bounds. This kind of enthusiasm, coupled with necessary research funds, succeeded in splitting the atom. Yet when science achieves a very high accuracy in a field that interests it less, the achievement leaves science cold, and often serves to put a valuable hypothesis on the shelf.

The Director of the Endocrine Research Clinic, Philadelphia, Dr. Michael J. Bennett, and Dr. P. B. Russell report in *The Southern Surgeon* that "the maternal ovaries play a most important part upon the incidence of premature births." The authors remark in passing, "we may mention here that it seems an easy matter to predict the cycle of the mature female and diagnose abnormal ovarian conditions by studying the vaginal smears [cellular fluctuations] of the young female previous to the onset of the menses or puberty." [25] If the menstrual-ovulatory cycle can be predicted in its general outlines even before menstruation or ovulation have begun, it looks as though the female cycle were not quite as unpredictable as reputed.

notes

CHAPTER ONE

How to Tell a Woman from a Man

[1] The newest thing in literature on the sexes is the concept of normality. If man would accept his essential maleness and woman her essential femaleness, it is asserted, misunderstanding and divorce would virtually cease. A "normal" male and a "normal" female will possess certain physical traits and lack certain others. If one possesses characteristics properly belonging to the opposite sex, one should "overcome" them, for they interfere with completeness, maturity, normality, and happiness. This key use of "normal" cannot be understood without studying the history of the word.

All sciences are concerned with accuracy of prediction: to make as many predictions as possible is a goal of science, and biology is no exception. To predict the behavior of lower animals of a given sex and species is far easier than to predict the behavior of men and women. Man is the unpredictable animal. The lower animals obey inherited instincts to a greater extent, and are therefore better all-around conformists than we.

Not only is their instinctual behavior more predictable and standardized, it is in general essential for the survival of the species. If a lactating rat does not display the maternal instinct, her young are likely to perish. If an animal does not react with appropriate instincts of self-preservation, it is likely to perish. Thus an animal with incompetent reflexes tends to be weeded out of the species: natural selection. *Conform or perish* seems to be a leading rule in the animal kingdom.

More individual animals fail to display appropriate instincts than is sometimes realized. However, exceptions are sufficiently rare to warrant the use of "normal" in describing their typical behavior. "A lactating rat normally displays a maternal instinct." *Normally* carries the linked meanings: (1) the phenomenon is very widespread within the given group; (2) the phenomenon is important for the survival of the species.

Biologists are not inclined to say, "The average lactating rat displays a maternal instinct." *Average* implies an adding together of various disparate elements, finding the arithmetical mean. But the behavior of the lower animals is more invariable than that. Further, "average" has a noncommittal quality. The biologist wants to suggest that what is *normal* is "important"—for the continuation of the species.

The word normal, equipped with these two meanings, has been taken over into the science of man and human biology. Sometimes we are told that the "average" male or the "average" female has such-and-such characteristics and not others; but it is equally common to hear that the "normal" male or female possesses them.

Keeping in mind the dual meaning of "normal," we will find that among primary and secondary sexual characteristics, some of the characteristics assigned to one sex and not the other will fulfill at least one requirement of the term "normal": they are widespread. Some of the characteristics will fulfill both requirements of "normal": they are widespread and also necessary for the continuation of the species. But other characteristics, numerically the greatest, are neither widespread within the given sex, nor necessary for survival of the species. These latter traits, then, represent what some writer *believes* are important or necessary for the species, or for society, or for the happiness of the individual.

The chief difference between the sexes is the difference in sex organs. These are indeed characteristics of the "normal" male and female. In fact, male and female possess such differences by definition. "Normal" is added to remind us that the difference is widespread and that the continuation of the species depends on it. So far the word normal is correctly used.

Another series of sex differences include such traits as more facial hair (a beard) in the case of the normal male, slightly greater height (three inches) than the average female, and so on. Characteristics of this type are (1) widespread within the given group, fulfilling one half of the word "normal"; but (2) they are not necessary for continuation of the species.

Yet there is no doubt that a note of "survival value," or desperate normality, has been infused into a description of these traits. So powerful is the psychological effect of the word normal, that a man in our society may feel thoroughly "male" only when in the presence of a woman shorter than himself. In the company of a woman taller, a man may feel "less male," somewhat de-masculinized, even feminized. One of the iniquities of the cult of normality is that a man in this case must either (gallantly) accept his own "abnormality," or conclude that the woman is "abnormally tall," somewhat "masculine." Heights vary appreciably in different parts of the country, both men and women being taller in the West. Thus a man may become progressively "less male" as he travels from New York to Wyoming; while a Western woman arriving in the East may suddenly feel a pronounced lack of "femininity."

Facial hair, another trait of this type, is widespread in the case of men, but varies considerably among individual men; and it is certainly not necessary for continuation of the species, as a race less hirsute than ours has amply demonstrated.

By far the largest and lengthiest group of "secondary

sex characteristics" includes such physical traits as broad
shoulders, square jaw, large muscles, bulging calves, and
any number of other attributes denoting what the "normal" male will wear. Here the use of "normal" is
definitely misleading. Normal implies a very widespread
condition: certain traits are to be present in one sex and
all but *absent in the other*. Normal implies survival
value: yet none of these traits are essential for continuation of the species.

So stringent are these lists of secondary sex characteristics that the vast majority of men and women in the
population are destined to be abnormal in some degree
or another, to possess characteristics properly belonging
to the opposite sex. For example, taking two traits expected of males, bulging calves and broad shoulders, it
may be that the "average" on calves was derived from
one Majority of males in the population, and the "average" on shoulders derived from another Majority. In
this event, only a very few men, literally exceptions,
can possess both counts of masculinity. Faced with a
whole set of such traits by which to adjudge one's normality, how many men will qualify for all the items: the
heavy brows *and* the big teeth *and* the thick neck *and*
the square shoulders *and* the large chest *and* the narrow
hips, and so on? Most men emerge with a "score" of 67
percent normality; 44 percent "completeness"; 30 percent "femininity," or what-you-will.

Still another ambiguity in lists of sex differences is
that the normal male is sometimes said to have shoulders
"broader" than the female's; at other times he is simply
said to have "broad shoulders." However, if a male is
described as having "broader" shoulders than the female,
and a female as having "more sloping, rounded" shoulders than the male, it is fair to conclude that the normal
male is expected to have shoulders *broad*-in-some-degree
and the normal female to have shoulders *rounded*-in-
some-degree. The habit of slipping from the specific

requirement to the comparative is convenient, if one is not to be embarrassed by the obvious incidence of broad shoulders in American women.

The distribution of these traits within the general population is suggested by the following sketch. The "masculine" traits are polarized at the right, the "feminine" traits at the left. Most of us possess some of each. That most of us are a mixture of these traits is proved not only by a casual walk down the street and a glance at one's fellows, but by a study made by William H. Sheldon and presented in *The Varieties of Human Physique* (Harper, 1940). In endomorphy (plumpness traits), mesomorphy (muscularity traits), and ectomorphy (vaguely—slenderness, fragility), men and women share in strikingly similar proportions. Cases of extreme muscularity are less frequent among women than among men, though they occur in both groups. Cases of extreme plumpness are slightly less frequent among men than among women. For example, Sheldon found 15 extremely plump women (out of 1000 women) and 8 extremely plump men (out of 1000 men). He found 14 extremely muscular men (out of 1000 men) and 4 extremely muscular women (out of 1000 women). The rectangles below therefore make more concession in terms of this sex difference than is actually required.

ALL FEMALES

Toward rounder chin, wider hips, smaller hands, etc.: the "female" physique

ALL MALES

Toward squarer jaw, thicker neck, broader shoulders, etc.: the "male" physique

Most of us reside in the shaded area. We have somewhat bulging calves but rounded shoulders, or broad shoulders and sloping rounded legs, etc. There is infinite variety in us.

Suppose that we decided to write a book on the differences between the sexes, not their similarities. We would find that if we "averaged up" the muscularity traits in the total male population, the results would show a slightly higher degree of muscularity than in the female population. The existence of a few *extreme* muscular types among males is enough to bring up the general average. Therefore we could state in our book, let us say, that the "average male" is more muscular than the "average female."

Next we might decide to illustrate these statistical findings. We would draw a sketch of an "average man" with the intention of pointing up the sexual "differences" between male and female. To make vivid the points of *dis*similarity, it is convenient to draw our "average male" from the unshaded area of the rectangle. He will be extremely muscular. Only a very small number of males in the population reflect this portrait. We call him "normal" because we like him, but he is by no means any longer the "average."

The same thing happens, with a greater degree of distortion, when we sketch the "average woman"—in order to show how she differs from the male. We do not ask: what are the proportions of the average woman, statistically derived from measurements; but we ask: in what special way do women differ from men? Adding all the measurements together and dividing by the number of women, we find a slightly higher degree of plumpness in women than in men. A few cases of extreme plumpness is enough to bring up the general average. Our sketch of the average-woman-who-differs-from-the-average-man now becomes a portrait of some woman out in the unshaded area. She has very wide hips, small hands, narrow shoulders, and so on. The majority of women do not look like her.

Thanks to the magical properties of the words "normal" and "average," our sketches of the average man and woman now give the reader an impression something like this:

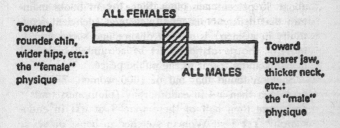

ALL FEMALES

Toward
rounder chin,
wider hips, etc.:
the "female"
physique

ALL MALES

Toward
squarer jaw,
thicker neck,
etc.:
the "male"
physique

in which the shaded area represents those individuals who "depart" from the presumed normal: the deviants. Since most of us live in the shaded area, the psychological effect of this sleight-of-hand is easily seen. We all think, in terms of the "average" man and woman, that we are "deviants."

Does the word Normal carry an implication of its opposite: that what does not measure up to the normal is extremely rare, and inimical to the species? If so, we have a right to know just *how rare* a departure from the Norm is. For it may be that we are being bullied by an imaginary Majority that really isn't there. When the biologist states what is "normal" among the lower animals, he is thinking of an 80 or 98 percent frequency. But the traits above, called "normal," are not found present in one sex and absent in the other with any such high frequency.

According to Sheldon (see Table 20, p. 127; Figure 13, p. 130), out of 1000 men only 14 will qualify as very high in all points of muscularity (mesomorphy). Degree of muscularity (as found in bulging calves,

"straight" arms, thick neck, and other traits) is estimated on a scale from 1 to 7. The "normal male" in
books on sex is generally a 7 in mesomorphy, certainly
never less than a 6. Yet 738 males out of 1000 (over
half) were not over a 4 in mesomorphy. Taking the
"muscular" traits alone, excluding the primary sex difference, most American men would find themselves
about 50 percent masculine. Since recent books maintain that deficient masculinity in men (deficient femininity in women) is causing divorce and social unrest,
most of the population must be accounted biological
deviants and a threat to the public peace.

Sheldon found that out of 1000 women, 755 were
no higher than a 4 in endomorphy (plumpness traits);
and more than half of these were 3 or less in endomorphy. Yet That Woman sketched in books on sex is
never less than a 5 in endomorphy, and more often she
is a 6. Again the majority of women in the population
must by this standard judge themselves inadequate,
masculinesque, and with more than enough to "overcome."

We must look beyond statistics and "survival of the
species" to discover why normality has become such a
vogue. There is an area of choice and an area of inevitability (or limitation of choice) in human lives, and
the continual danger is that areas of choice will be suppressed by claims of "inevitability." Thus recent theo-
ries are anxious to define the realm of activities and
emotions which will, for the Normal woman, become
mandatory. Since these normalities are based not only
on the difference in primary sex organs but on a difference between men and women as regards musculature,
fat content, bone structure, and all sorts of other cri-
teria, it is important that these facts be presented correctly and with a minimum of confusion.

To indicate one of the unkind uses to which the word
"abnormal" is put, we might consider a phenomenon

important to women: sterility. Sterility occurs among
the lower animals and also among humans, of both
sexes. Few biologists would hesitate to say that sterility
was abnormal in a woman of childbearing age. Very
well, "abnormal" suggests that sterility is extremely rare
among women of childbearing age, and that it is inimical to the continuance of the species. Yet is either
of these precisely involved? Facts show that 10 percent
of women of childbearing age are sterile. Is this "extremely rare" or just "infrequent"? One out of every
ten makes a sizeable number. Further, is sterility in one
woman out of ten a genuine threat to the species? The
hurling of "abnormal" is here merely a form of verbal
witch-burning.

Considering "normality" as an ideal, it is interesting
to note a marked divergence between the biologist's
ideal woman and everyone else's. Powers models are almost the antithesis of a "normal female." Few movie
stars conform to the proper wrestler-male physique or
the "motherly"-female physique. Jane Russell is perhaps
the best representative of "normal femininity" in Hollywood, and she has had difficulty getting past the cen-
sors.

Does "normal" indicate statistical frequency? Not always.

Does "normal" indicate "survival value"? Not necessarily.

Does "normal" outline an ideal? It frequently does.
And if so, we should discuss such ideals, re the democratic privilege. For ideals guide society in its course,
and must not be handed down from above but be
evolved from the actual human needs of the people involved.

In conclusion it might be pointed out that while, from
one generation to the next, a scrupulous distinction between male and female is preserved, nature has by no
means seen fit to keep broad shoulders confined to the

male of the species or wide hips to the female. In fact,
if a 100 percent pure and complete male (of the unshaded area) were to wed a 100 percent pure and
complete female (of the unshaded area), there is no
guarantee that the son of such a union might not inherit
wide hips and the daughter broad shoulders. These unfortunate children, produced by exemplary parents and
reminded of the same, are presumably to learn from
biology manuals that they are a similar disappointment
to the species.

CHAPTER TWO

Josie Takes the Stand

[1] This account is freely adapted from Robert M.
Yerkes' *Chimpanzees* (Yale University, 1943), Chapter
Five, entitled "Male and Female." This was a popular
presentation of the experiment. However, criticism can
also be leveled at a technical presentation of the experiment: "Social Behavior of Chimpanzees: Dominance between Mates, in Relation to Sexual Status" by R. M.
Yerkes in the *Journal of Comparative Psychology*, v. 30,
1940, pp. 147-86. Here Yerkes reports that after testing
a large number of pairs, the results were statistically dis-
appointing. "To select a variety of cycle as typical except
on the basis of frequency of occurrence must seem inde-
fensibly arbitrary. We therefore have chosen, as alternative procedure, to define typical by characteristics of subjects and pair instead of by cycle data. Accordingly, we
shall, for present purposes, consider typical the behavior
of adult, sexually and reproductively normal and experienced, acquainted and congenial, moderately self-confi-
dent and self-assertive individuals and pairs." Pp. 176-77.

This decision to define *the typical* by something other
than frequency of occurrence involves the elimination of

a quantity of data on the behavior of certain subjects, presumed atypical. Most revealing for our purposes is the elimination of all observations "for Lia and Pati [two females] because they are highly dominant."

The prostitution hypothesis seems to have suffered from one Nira, a female who refused to mate, and thus to exchange favors, but who nevertheless took over the food chute. And Lia, though scarcely more than half Jack's size, dominated the food chute after detumescence; yet sex relations were never observed between them. The latter case, Yerkes remarks, "exemplifies the relative deadliness of the female!"

The reasons for the addition of the terms *right* and *privilege* to the discussion of the experiment are of interest: page 179 of this article.

[2] R. M. Yerkes and J. H. Elder: "Oestrus, Receptivity, and Mating in Chimpanzee," *Comparative Psychology Monographs*, v. 13, October, 1936, p. 10. In discussing whether it is not the female who almost entirely controls the sex relation, the authors write: "The female ignores his solicitations if she sees fit; terminates the sexual union when she will—and that may be before orgasm and completion of ejaculation." In 1939 in an article in the *Quarterly Review of Biology* (v. 36, p. 135), Yerkes mentions in passing, "rape by the male," but gives no further explanation or reference. The two females mentioned in *Chimpanzees* (p. 65) who refused to mate did not suffer rape apparently.

CHAPTER THREE

Is Rape a Myth?

[1] "The dynamic essence of the masculine spirit, based perhaps chiefly on biological functions, has been described as the impulse to penetrate, to make an impress

upon something or someone. It is this that leads to
clashes between men, this that leads to the happy union
of the receptive female and the propulsive male." Karl
Menninger, with the collaboration of Jeanetta Lyle Menninger: *Love against Hate* (Allen & Unwin, 1942), p.
106.

[2] *Ibid.*, p. 113. A woman's personality is predicated
on that of her husband's for by "protecting or building
up the personality of her husband or lover by means of
her receptivity, the woman builds her own personality."
P. 107.

[3] Amram Scheinfeld: *Women and Men* (Chatto &
Windus, 1943), p. 249.

CHAPTER FOUR

A Minor Mystery

[1] Dr. Helena B. Wright: *The Sex Factor in Marriage*
(Vanguard, 1938). This is an excellent handbook, probably the best in its field; it is all the more interesting to
see the subtle way in which the sensations of the clitoris
are subordinated to those of the vagina as the discussion
turns from a consideration of anatomy to "adjustment."
On page 67 we find, "Its anatomical name is the
clitoris. This little organ is capable of giving the most
acute sensations." On page 68, "The moist membrane
lining the vagina is an important seat of sensations that
differ in kind from the sensations of the clitoris, but are
capable of an almost equal acuteness." On page 91, "As
a general rule it is true to say that a woman has not at-
tained fullest sex experience until she is able to feel
pleasure as acutely in the vagina as in the region of the
clitoris." And on page 114, "in perfect marital stimulation the vaginal sensation predominates."

[2] R. L. Dickinson: *Human Sex Anatomy, A Topographical Hand Atlas* (Baillière, Tindall & Cox, 1933), p. 42.

Cf. Dr. Frederick J. Taussig's statement: "The nerves originate from the internal pudenda and three large branches run to the clitoris, a greater amount than that which supplies the penis. The glans contains numerous pacchionian bodies and extensive nerve filaments. Hence this structure is hypersensitive." *Gynecological and Obstetrical Monographs,* v. 13, 1931, p. 22.

"The size of the clitoris," writes Dr. Dickinson in the text cited above, "varies considerably, with small apparent relation to general body dimensions, and seems also relatively little affected by external events. . . . One learns to ask, not what is 'average' or 'normal' but rather 'what is the most common dimension or grouping?' That is, the true measure is the *mode* rather than the arithmetical *average* or *mean.* . . . The most usual lengthwise diameter is 4 to 5 mm. with the transverse grouped a little lower, from 3 to 4 mm. The relatively high 'average' figures quoted [by others] are probably affected by the presence in the various lists of inter-sex individuals, whose unusual appearance would lead to the taking of measurement." *Op. cit.,* p. 45.

"Again, size is not necessarily a criterion of responsiveness. A very tiny clitoris . . . may be associated with powerful orgasm from friction or pressure on the organ alone. The other extreme in bulk is found in intersex individuals whose sexual impulse and activity is usually strongly developed. With women at sixty or seventy the clitoris may be prominent and large." P. 46.

[3] Dickinson, *Human Sex Anatomy,* p. 86.

[4] Dickinson and Lura Beam, *A Thousand Marriages* (Baillière, Tindall & Cox, 1931), p. 63.

[5] Dickinson, *Human Sex Anatomy,* p. 86.

[6] Sigmund Freud: *Introductory Lectures on Psychoanalysis* (Allen & Unwin, 1935), p. 278.

CHAPTER FIVE

Love at Bay

[1] *Cf.* Karl Menninger: *Love against Hate.* "Many men baselessly accuse their wives of frigidity: the wife would like to respond but she is not permitted to; she is not given time to; her efforts are not acknowledged—sometimes they are even strongly disapproved. But a boy cannot conceive of his mother approving or co-operating in his sexual activities, and a man who marries a woman who represents his mother is in precisely this dilemma." P. 75.

[2] Dr. Fritz Kahn in his book *Our Sex Life* (Heinemann, 1953) devotes one paragraph to "*The sexual hygiene of the man,*" while thirteen pages are devoted to an explanation of the complicated hygiene of the woman. The author is himself conscious of this disproportionate emphasis, and explains it in this way:

The woman is obliged to take special care since:

1. The woman's genitals are the seat of sweat and odour glands, which secrete particularly strongly (organs of attraction!).

2. The foreskin of the clitoris secretes a sebaceous matter, like that of the man, which easily becomes rancid and then has a foul odour.

3. The vagina secretes a fluid with a sour odour, which dirties the skin and underwear upon increased secretion.

4. The urethra ends in a concealed spot, so that traces of urine remain and can spread the foul odour of decomposed urine. P. 164.

These four descriptive items are supposed to explain why the hygiene of woman differs from the hygiene of man and requires twenty-six times more discussion. Yet no one of these "differences" distinguishes women. The first two items apply to men as well as to women. In analogy to the third, the penis secretes a fluid with similar potentialities. In the fourth, the male is equally subject to these horrendous results.

What is important is the decided communication of "uncleanliness" in the list. In spite of the parenthetical "organs of attraction!" the subsequent appraisive terms, "rancid," "foul," "sour," "dirties," "decomposed" dissipate any attitude of tolerance. In the paragraph devoted to male hygiene there is a complete absence of such terms. The male is given certain simple directives relating to ordinary cleanliness, soap and water. And why? In order to avoid uncomfortable irritations or—after contact with a woman—"the possibility of an infection."

CHAPTER SIX

Witchcraft and the Moon

[1] Dr. Isabel Emslie Hutton: *The Sex Technique in Marriage* (Emerson, 1938), p. 126.

[2] Boris B. Rubenstein: "The Vaginal Smear—Basal Body Temperature Technic and its Application to the Study of Functional Sterility in Woman," *Endocrinology*, v. 27, 1940, p. 855.

[3] Fritz Kahn: *Our Sex Life.* "The entire mental constitution of the woman, together with her sexual character and her fertility, fluctuates with the monthly rhythm of her ovarian function." P. 44.

[4] Kenneth Walker: *The Physiology of Sex* (Pelican, 1942), p. 64. "Havelock Ellis has even suggested that feminine modesty may be traced back to this sexual periodicity. Looked at from this point of view modesty may be said to be the escape from male attention of a female who is not yet at the period of oestrus. When, however, modesty overlaps the period of heat it meets

the impact of sexuality, thus producing the behaviour known as coquetry. In this the female alternately approaches and runs away from the male, thereby fanning her wooer's ardour." Pp. 64-65.

[5] R. L. Dickinson and Lura Beam: *A Thousand Marriages*, p. 64.

CHAPTER SEVEN

What Shall We Do with the Climacteric?

[1] Ernest R. Groves: *Marriage* (Henry Holt, 1933), pp. 482; 479. "In the case of the woman the most important change is that which appears in the ovaries, which gradually diminish in size and wither away until only a remnant is left." P. 479.

[2] R. L. Dickinson: *Human Sex Anatomy*, Fig. 125.

[3] National Resources Planning Board: "Human Conservation; the Story of Our Wasted Resources," March 1943 (U.S. Govt. Printing Office). "Recent estimates indicate that probably 10 percent of all marriages may be sterile because of some factor affecting the reproductive capacity of either the husband or the wife. Sometimes sterility occurs after the first or second child has been born and prevents further childbearing." P. 8.

[4] George Gellhorn: "Non-Operative Treatment in Gynecology," *Gynecological and Obstetrical Monographs*, v. 14, 1924, p. 252.

[5] Fritz Kahn: *Our Sex Life*, pp. 211-12. Other references in this section refer to his chapter, "Sterility," pp. 211-24.

[6] *Ibid.*, pp. 257-59.

[7] Abner I. Weisman: "The Effect of Temperature upon the Vitality of Spermatozoa," *American Journal of Obstetrics and Gynecology*, v. 38, 1939, p. 313.

[8] William H. Cary and Robert L. Dickinson, "Ste-

rility and Conception," *Gynecological and Obstetrical Monographs*, v. 20, 1928, p. 2.

CHAPTER EIGHT

Society Writes Biology

[1] Fritz Kahn: *Our Sex Life*, p. 256.

[2] *Ibid.*, p. 55.

[3] Kenneth Walker: *The Physiology of Sex*, p. 28.

[4] Fritz Kahn, *Our Sex Life*, p. 6.

[5] *Ibid.*, p. 29.

[6] H. M. Parshley: *The Science of Human Reproduction* (Norton, 1933), p. 106.

[7] Amram Scheinfeld: *Women and Men*, pp. 233-34.

[8] *Ibid.*, p. 234.

[9] Kenneth Walker: *The Physiology of Sex*, p. 40.

[10] The matriarchal biologist uses Walker's data (see note 3 above) but draws an opposite conclusion.

[11] *Cf.* Van de Velde's description of semen.

[12] *Cf.* I. E. Hutton: *The Sex Technique in Marriage.* "There are innumerable spermatozoa contained in the tubules of the testes, and their formation goes on constantly. They are composed of very rich and highly-specialized material." Pp. 67-68.

H. B. Wright: *The Sex Factor in Marriage.* "The male life-cell, however, as well as being round, possesses the finest possible tail, by means of which it has the power of wriggling itself along on a moist surface. The female life-cell has no power of movement by itself—it has to be moved by some force outside it." P. 55.

[13] Fritz Kahn supplies this highly provocative paragraph in *Our Sex Life*, p. 85. Authorities are not in agreement on this point.

[14] *Ibid.*, illustration note facing p. 189.

[15] *Cf.* notes 7 and 8 above, relating to the patriarchal account.

CHAPTER NINE

And Then They Were One

[1] As reported by R. L. Dickinson in "The Average Sex Life of American Women," *Journal of the American Medical Association*, v. 85, 1925. "To judge by known cases, a fourth continued the practice after marriage." That is, of the married women who reported autoerotic practices at one time or another in their lives, a fourth of these stated that they had continued after marriage. P. 1115.

CHAPTER TEN

The Good Will Hour

[1] This barefaced preference for *drive* over *comfort* is nothing more than a mesomorphic bias. In terms of constitutional psychology, the present book is an attempt to exonerate the mesomorphic component in women. The endomorphic and ectomorphic components have always found acceptance. They alone have entered into the definition of true femininity, while the mesomorphic factor has been tacitly excluded as non-feminine, or even masculine. With the further development of constitutional psychology and the study of women, many of the current injustices will be dissolved, for if mesomorphy turns up as frequently in women as endomorphy or ectomorphy, it deserves a place in any definition of "true femininity."

See William H. Sheldon: *The Varieties of Human*

Physique (Harper, 1940) and *The Varieties of Temperament* (Harper, 1942).

2 R. L. Dickinson: *Human Sex Anatomy*, p. 86.

3 The usual position today is called the "modern" position. Fritz Kahn: *Our Sex Life*, pp. 77-78.

4 Oliver M. Butterfield: *Marriage and Sexual Harmony* (Emerson, 1936), p. 11.

5 Two of R. L. Dickinson's major works, not mentioned elsewhere in these notes, are *The Single Woman; a Medical Study in Sex Education* (Williams and Norgate, 1934) and the remarkable *Birth Atlas*, reproductions of twenty-four life-size sculptures of fertilization, growth, stages of labor and involution, by Dickinson and Abram Belskie (Maternity Center Association, N. Y., 3d ed., 1947).

CHAPTER ELEVEN

A New Generation

1 While Freud knew the nerve endings of the clitoris were equivalent to those of the penis, he nevertheless permitted the concept of the organic inferiority of the female, in respect to her capacity for sexual enjoyment, to take a central place in his writings.

Cf., Gregory Zilboorg: "Masculine and Feminine," *Psychiatry*, v. 7, 1944. "The organic inferiority of woman, as Freud put it, and the superiority of man, both implied and asserted in psychoanalytic theory. . . ." P. 259.

2 Reported by R. L. Dickinson: "The Average Sex Life of American Women," *Journal of the American Medical Association*, v. 85, 1925. "The practice commenced for the most part between the ages of 5 and 11 (42 percent), that is, well in advance of puberty, while before reaching 16 nearly 60 percent of those practicing had begun. The mode or peak of the beginnings is

at the eighth year. Herein lies a notable contrast between male and female, since three fourths of the males
start between 12 and 17. As for orgasm, though the
term was not always understood, it seems to be late in
developing, since its appearance is listed, in 62 percent
of those reporting, as beginning at or after the eight-
eenth year." P. 1114.

3 V. 20, 1893, p. 645. For an interesting stenographic
report of the meeting of the London Obstetrical Society
in which Dr. Brown was voted out of the society (after
making his defense), see *Medical Times and Gazette*
(London), v. 1, 1867, pp. 366-78; or *British Medical
Journal*, v. 1, 1867, pp. 395-410.

4 *Journal of the American Medical Association*, v. 8,
1887, pp. 441-42.

5 V. 56, 1907, pp. 742-43.

6 Rowland G. Freeman: "Circumcision in Masturbation in Female Infants," *American Journal of Obstetrics*,
v. 70, 1914, pp. 315-16.

7 R. L. Dickinson: *Human Sex Anatomy*, p. 46.

CHAPTER TWELVE

Education for Frigidity

1 H. C. Bingham: "Sex Development in Apes," *Comparative Psychology Monographs*, v. 5, May, 1928, pp.
1-165. The quotations from Dr. Bingham are taken
from this monograph.

CHAPTER THIRTEEN

The Laws of Rapture

1 Walter B. Cannon: *Bodily Changes in Pain, Hunger, Fear and Rage* (D. Appleton, 1915). "The re-

searches here reported have revealed a number of un-suspected ways in which muscular action is made more efficient because of emotional disturbances of the viscera. Every one of the visceral changes that have been noted —the cessation of processes in the alimentary canal (thus freeing the energy supply for other parts); the shifting of blood from the abdominal organs, whose activities are deferable, to the organs immediately essential to muscular exertion (the lungs, the heart, the central nervous system); the increased vigor of contraction of the heart; the quick abolition of the effects of muscular fatigue, the mobilizing of energy-giving sugar in the circulation—every one of these visceral changes is *directly serviceable in making the organism more effective in the violent display of energy which fear or rage or pain [or intense excitement] may involve.*" Pp. 215-16.

Cannon was primarily concerned with the antagonistic action of the cranial and the sympathetic nervous systems, the nerves which govern digestion and those that prepare the body for struggle or escape. When he turned for brief comment to the emotions of sex, he noted a similar antagonism between the sacral nervous system (controlling erection) and the sympathetic nervous system. That is, the sacral he called "the servant of racial continuity," and its impulses were opposed, in any given organ, to those of the sympathetic nervous system.

However, Cannon was hard put to explain why intense sexual excitement did not therefore cancel out erection; or how it was that the sympathetic system should be called in for ejaculation and orgasm. It was Cannon's belief that the sacral dominated the early portion of the sex act, while "the completion of the process—the contractions of the seminal vesicles and the prostate, and the subsidence of engorged tissues" was brought about by the sympathetic nervous system, which appeared to overwhelm the sacral nervous discharges.

The laws of rapture which are recounted in Chapter XIII are based on a premise that Cannon did not subscribe to: that sex is a major emotion and thus activates the sympathetic nervous system in ways similar to other major emotions, fear, pain and rage.

Whether sex is "characteristically" sacral or sympathetic, or even cranial, may devolve upon temperamental differences between individuals. For the endomorph, sex may have relatively more in common with digestive and cranial functions. Love is by one school of thought illustrated by analogies to food: love as a banquet, i.e., "the upbuilder and restorer of the organic reserves." For the ectomorph, comparatively "nerve"-dominated, sex may involve greater intensity and less duration, possessing fewer "digestive" or "muscular" attributes. For the mesomorph with his enthusiasm for muscular exhilaration, a note of excitement may dominate. In this case the sympathetic nervous system would play a central role, bringing with it the cessation of digestion, acceleration of the heart, quick abolition of fatigue, mobilizing of energy, and a sense of motor efficiency.

Cannon writes that when feelings grow very intense, the responses of the sympathetic nervous system become remarkably uniform; "under such conditions the identity of these responses with those characteristically aroused in the belligerent emotion of anger or rage and its counterpart, fear, offer interesting possibilities of transformation and substitution" (p. 285). Darwin wrote, "In the agony of pain almost every muscle of the body is brought into strong action" (Cannon, p. 189). The latter might serve to explain why a mesomorph often displays an indifference to pain that seems "abnormal" to other individuals. The sense of having "almost every muscle of the body" called into play is for him strongly compensatory.

Unless we are willing to study the different needs of

different individuals it is impossible to understand or remedy individual frustrations.

[2] *Cf.* Cannon (*Ibid.*, p. 219), "it is of interest to note that on occasions when great demands are likely to be placed on the neuro-muscular system in the doing of unusual labors, emotional excitement is not uncommonly an accompaniment."

Since emotional excitement automatically puts the skeletal muscles on the *qui vive* it is one step toward "the doing of unusual labors." A society exercises censorship not only over the *acts* of its citizens but over the *enthusiasms* of its citizens. The more alternatives of action the society allows, the greater the variety of enthusiasms it permits.

[3] The female chimpanzee indulges in a curious sort of skeletal rigidity before coition. Stiffening arms and legs, this behavior is a form of active exertion, the pitting of one set of skeletal muscles against another, with all the inner effects of activity, energy, and excitement but without external motion.

[4] Cannon, *ibid.* "What rest will do only after an hour or more, adrenin will do in five minutes or less." P. 133.

[5] Jules H. Masserman: *Behavior and Neurosis* (University of Chicago, 1943), p. 204.

CHAPTER FOURTEEN

Women as Something Special

[1] "Sex and Character," *Psychiatry*, v. 6, February, 1943, p. 31.

[2] John Dollard: *Caste and Class in a Southern Town* (Yale University, 1937), Chapter XII, "Accommodation Attitudes of Negroes," pp. 250-66. A few additional quotations and some comments on their application to women may help clarify these minority-group mores.

The imitation of the speech of Negroes, writes Dollard, always gives *an image of a high-toned, pleading voice, full of uncertainty, begging for favor. Evidently this whining, cajoling tone is one of the badges of inferiority which Negroes accept and cultivate.* Cf., women, who not only have a naturally high-pitched voice but often cultivate a supplicatory whining intonation. That a woman often employs this tone to a man rather than to a woman (except a rival) indicates its practical use in conciliation.

The white caste is quite aware of what it wants in Negroes. It idealizes the "old-timy" Negroes . . . the bandana around the head, the Sambo and Rastus types, belief in spells and conjures, love of their white folks, and a highly cultivated white-folks manner. In short the phrase is a direct reference to the slavery Negro of the well-accommodated, house-servant type. Cf., the idealization of the "real" woman, duly submissive, with a cultivated men-folks manner, not infrequently a well-accommodated house-servant type.

It should be noted that these ["old-timy"] *Negroes had their primary allegiance to the single, masterful white man . . . not . . . to the sibling caste members.* Cf., the cattiness and disloyalty to other women expected of a "really feminine" woman in our culture.

An informant . . . has referred to the Negro as a "Dr. Jekyll and Mr. Hyde." He was making an observation that is well understood among Negroes—that he has a kind of dual personality, two roles, one that he is forced to play with white people, and one . . . as he appears in his dealings with his own people. What the white southern people see who "know their Negroes" is the role that they have forced the Negro to accept, his caste role. . . . It is perhaps this fact which often makes Negroes seem so deceptive to white people. Cf., the dominant male who both "knows his women" and generally finds them "variable," unpredictable, unreasonable, and deceptive.

Negroes become quite adept both at concealing their feelings and dealing with white people. A Negro informant said that Negroes learn to get along with white people by outwitting them, by studying them closely, and by marking the points at which they are susceptible to influence. Cf., the cleverness, indirection, and "feminine wiles" by which women are expected to achieve their goals.

The value of accommodation is actively propagandized within the Negro group. Cf., the Women's Page in newspapers, and the advice to the lovelorn advising tact, diplomacy, and an appearance of helplessness in getting one's way; a candid request, women are told, will get them nowhere: make the man think it was his idea in the first place.

[3] Jules H. Masserman: *Behavior and Neurosis.* The quotations on the cats are from pages 69, 89, 107, and 159. If we examine the reactions of these animals to an insecure and conflictful situation, we find some of the "feminine" traits of women: the preening and desire for fondling, the vocalizing plaintively, the exaggerated and ludicrous playfulness or coquetry, the mannerisms, and so on. If we examine these "insecure" attributes we find some of the same traits ascribed to the underprivileged Negro in the South: the marked "startle responses" (the standard Hollywood caricature), exaggerated and ludicrous playfulness, mannerisms, and so on.

[4] A minority group will find itself encouraged in the building of churches and discouraged in the building of schools. As Dollard writes, "Improvements for Negroes, such as a school building, do not just happen. The white people have to be shown how it is to their advantage." P. 262. Cf., the following note 5.

Over one hundred years ago Stendhal observed: "We

have seen a law carried in the United States, in 1818, which condemns to thirty-four strokes of the cat anyone teaching a Virginian Negro to read. Nothing could be more consequent and more reasonable than a law of this kind. Were the United States of America themselves more useful to the motherland when they were her slaves or since they have become her equals?"

[5] The promises of modern advertising are reminiscent of magical formulas. *Cf.*, Dollard, "The plain purpose of the magical act as seen in the life-history context is to gratify some wish, for love, revenge, or power, which is not attainable in the person's actual life. The existence of such practices among Negroes is by no mean displeasing, apparently, to white people; magical arts probably tend to absorb some of the discontent which would otherwise be directed at the system itself." P. 264.

CHAPTER FIFTEEN

A World of Differences

[1] R. L. Dickinson: "Requirements for an Ideal Contraceptive," *Human Fertility*, v. 5, 1940, pp. 162-63.

[2] Nicholas J. Eastman: "The Aims of Birth Control and Their Place in Preventive Medicine," *New International Clinics*, v. 1, 1942, pp. 271-306.

"Although improvements in obstetrics have made gratifying inroads on maternal mortality, there remain a large number of deaths in childbearing which occur because the women are unfit subjects for pregnancy as the result of chronic disease processes. Reliable and conservative estimates indicate that such fatalities make up one-fourth of all our maternal deaths. Great multiparity is another important cause of death in childbearing since the mortality rate doubles after the sixth child. In addition to these actual deaths, the amount of invalidism in both of these groups which pregnancy produces or aggravates, is incalculable. Obviously, any attempt to improve the plight of these mothers must depend on some form of contraception." P. 272.

"Of the more than two million births which take place in the United States yearly, a million occur in families on relief or with an income of less than $1,000 a year; approximately 900,000 births occur in families on relief or with an income of less than $800 a year." P. 273.

[8] E. C. Tolman: *Drives toward War* (Appleton-Century, 1942), p. 14.

[4] Havelock Ellis: "The Changing Status," in *The Woman Question*, ed. T. R. Smith (Boni and Liveright [1918]), pp. 227-28.

[5] Amram Scheinfeld: *Women and Men*, p. 376. Scheinfeld is arguing this in terms of the *Gestalt* concept of personality: "To the extent that you differ from any other person in one or more traits, all your traits would in some measure be different," p. 376. Yet why should the construction of the sex organs be the determining trait? On the basis of constitutional psychology one might argue that all broad-shouldered individuals, of whatever sex, will be in temperament and personality unlike all rounded-shouldered individuals; for this too is a trait. There are many other discernible traits in human beings, blue eyes and brown, height and weight. If society accorded one type of training to blue-eyed persons and another type to brown-eyed, it might be possible to say after a time that "every blue-eyed person must be in temperament and personality unlike all brown-eyed persons in various important ways." Since human beings possess inumerable traits, it would be interesting to know which traits were exercising a major influence on personality and behavior. Scheinfeld's hierarchical arrangement of these, with masculinity and femininity at the top, is the conventional picture only.

CHAPTER SIXTEEN

Here Are the Facts

[1] William Walter Greulich, Edward S. Morris, and Marion E. Black: "The Age of Corpora Lutea and Timing of Ovulation," in *Proceedings of the Conference on Problems of Human Fertility*, Sponsored by the National Committee on Maternal Health, January 15-16, 1943, New York City, ed. by Earl T. Engle (George Banta, Menasha, Wis., 1943), pp. 37-66. The subjects were hospitalized women who led regular lives; their temperatures were obtained daily. After one or two complete menstrual cycles had been studied, the operations were performed according to a definite schedule: some at the point of lowest temperature, others after the sharp drop had begun to rise. As the investigators put it, "We have had an opportunity to check at laparotomy the validity of changes in basal body temperature as an indication of ovulation." P. 41.

In their summary appears this statement: "In at least six of our cases in which we deliberately scheduled the operation after the drop in temperature had occurred but before the subsequent rise had begun, no ovulation had occurred. This proves that the drop in temperature itself is not necessarily accompanied by ovulation. With only very few exceptions, those cases in which both the drop in temperature and a subsequent rise had occurred, ovulation was also found to have taken place," p. 60. In these predictions, only one of the clues was used: temperature fluctuation. Other studies and predictions have been made solely on the basis of cellular fluctuations. When these two indices are taken together, and checked against one another, the accuracy is increased.

[2] Richard J. Blandau and William C. Young: "The

Effects of Delayed Fertilization on the Development of the Guinea Pig Ovum," *American Journal of Anatomy*, v. 64, 1939, pp. 303-29. This report does not concern itself with application to man except in the following statement: "Whether or not the time of fertilization with respect to ovulation is of importance for embryonic development in man is not known. On the other hand, the possibility cannot be excluded and is one that should be considered. In man the ratio of very early to late abortions is high. According to Taussig, 9 percent of 3060 spontaneous abortions occurred during the first month of pregnancy, 42 percent during the second month, 32 percent during the third month, and 17 percent during the remaining months. Schwalbe expresses the opinion that the relative number of abortions during the first month is more numerous than that usually given in compiled tables. It may be, partly because no definite heat period occurs in man, that eggs which have been in the tubes for sometime are occasionally fertilized and undergo a short period of abnormal development which is followed by intra-uterine reabsorption or abortion." P. 316.

Also see Richard J. Blandau and Edwin S. Jordan: "The Effect of Delayed Fertilization on the Development of the Rat Ovum," *American Journal of Anatomy*, v. 68, 1941, pp. 275-91.

[8] Nicholas J. Eastman: "The Aims of Birth Control and their Place in Preventive Medicine," *New International Clinics*, v. 1, 1942: "the most common cause of miscarriage is defective germ plasm," p. 295. Particularly in very pathological ova where almost no development of the embryo has taken place, the term *germ plasm deficiency* is used to account for the miscarriage.

[4] For the lower primates it is advisable that mates be kept together during the whole oestrous period rather than for only a short time when ovulation is believed to be taking place. In terms of the guinea pig experiment,

"single matings would be hazardous unless properly
timed in relation to the process of ovulation." Robert
M. Yerkes: *Chimpanzees*, p. 242.

These hazardous single matings without regard to
time of ovulation are, of course, the typical circumstances under which human beings are conceived.

[5] Here are some of the results as adapted from Table
1, Blandau and Young: "The Effects of Delayed Fertilization on the Development of the Guinea Pig
Ovum," *op. cit.*, p. 308.

Time when Inseminated	Percentage of Animals that Became Pregnant	Percentage of Normal Pregnancies	Percentage of Abnormal Pregnancies
During heat (prior to ovulation)	83	88	12
8 hours after ovulation....	67	66	34
14 hours after ovulation....	56	27	73
20 hours after ovulation....	31	10	90
26 hours after ovulation....	7	0	100
32 hours after ovulation....	0	0	0

[6] For sheer variability there is little to equal the menstrual-ovulatory cycles of functionally sterile women. The
cycles of normal women are generally considered too
"irregular" to study; but the cycles of functionally sterile
women are frequently discerned and therapy administered accordingly.

An interesting article in this connection is Dr. Boris
B. Rubenstein's "The Vaginal Smear-Basal Body Temperature Technic and Its Application to the Study of
Functional Sterility in Women" in *Endocrinology*, v.
27, 1940, pp. 843-56. "It should be noted," he writes,
"that usually the vaginal smear [cellular fluctuations of
the mucosa] and basal rectal temperatures will show a
discrepancy when some nongonadal influence affects one
or the other, thus the combination of the two methods
avoids in large part the unreliability of either method
alone." P. 851.

7 Arnold L. Soderwall and Richard J. Blandau: "The Duration of the Fertilizing Capacity of Spermatozoa in the Female Genital Tract of the Rat," *Journal of Experimental Zoology*, v. 88, 1941, pp. 55-64. In this experiment there happened to be no abnormal pregnancies in either the control or the experimental group.

8 Franklin P. Mall: "The Pathology of the Human Ovum," in *Manual of Human Embryology*, ed. by Franz Keibel and F. P. Mall (Lippincott, 1910), Vol. I, p. 205.

9 "Monsters of all varieties and of all degrees of intensity are produced in the first months of pregnancy. As a rule, the changes in them are so radical that they lead to their own destruction and they are aborted." *Ibid.*, p. 207.

10 "It has been my aim to demonstrate that the embryos found in pathological human ova and those obtained experimentally in animals are not analogous or similar, but identical. A double monster or a cyclopean fish is identical with the same condition in human beings. In all cases, monsters are produced by external influences acting upon the ovum," p. 69. F. P. Mall: "On the Frequency of Localized Anomalies in Human Embryos and Infants at Birth," *American Journal of Anatomy*, v. 22, 1917, pp. 49-72.

11 Nicholas J. Eastman: "Habitual Abortion," in *Progress in Gynecology*, ed. by Joe V. Meigs and Somers H. Sturgis (Grune and Stratton, N. Y., 1946), p. 264.

12 *Ibid.*, p. 262. Mall anticipated a marked difference in the ratio of pathological embryos according to "different communities and in different classes of society," but Eastman states (1946): "Neither race, social status, nor parity seems to effect this incidence."

On the basis of the spontaneous cure rate, incidentally, Eastman questions some of the reports that progesterone therapy is efficacious in treating habitual abortion. The progesterone deficiency theory is "the basis for most treatment" in cases of successive miscarriage, although it is "virtually impossible," he writes, to prove that the decreased pregnandiol output a few days before the aborton is what caused the death of the embryo; the death of the embryo may have caused the decreased output. Reports of success of therapy based on this theory, he notes, have generally considered habitual abortion as two or more spontaneous, consecutive abortions, but the spontaneous cure rate alone can account for over 60 percent of these recoveries. Hence any convincing proof would require "salvage rates of well over 75 percent." *Ibid.*, p. 265.

This doubt regarding a standard therapy is significant, for it indicates that most treatment of abortions attributed to maternal factors is being administered in terms of a theory which it is admittedly impossible to prove. The delayed fertilization hypothesis is no more doubtful than the progesterone deficiency theory, and the former is at least susceptible to empirical corroboration or disproof.

Another diagnosis of a maternal factor is that Vitamin E deficiency causes repeated abortion. This hypothesis Eastman also casts doubt on for various reasons, one being that human diets are rarely deficient in Vitamin E. He does not refer to the possibility of a delayed fertilization factor in abortion.

[13] Physicians continually warn against the laity's treating miscarriage too lightly. Medical care and rest are required. The danger of hemorrhage appears to be less than the danger of septic complications, as when some of the foetal products remain. See Frederick J. Lynch: "The Treatment of Miscarriage and Septic Abortion," in *Progress in Gynecology*, pp. 308-12.

[14] "Most pregnancies which ended before the twenty-seventh day and probably some pregnancies which ended between the twenty-seventh and fifty-fifth days can be attributed to delayed fertilization. Abortions after this

time were as common in the control group as in the experimental group and are attributed to other causes."
Blandau and Young: "The Effects of Delayed Fertilization on the Development of the Guinea Pig Ovum,"
op. cit., p. 317.

[15] "Rapid loss of the ability to be fertilized, retarda-
tion in the rate of development, and the occurrence of
many structural abnormalities have been described following the late fertilization of several species of sea
urchins, the marine annelid . . . the rainbow trout, and
the frog [references include studies from 1900 to 1934]."
Ibid., p. 315. Since in these species, maternal factors are
eliminated, Blandau and Young point out the probability that age of ovum has influenced the course of
development. "It is not to be assumed of course that
age at the time of fertilization is the only factor which
might make an ovum defective, but it appears to be one
which could easily be involved." *Ibid.*, p. 316.

[16] F. P. Mall: "On the Frequency of Localized Anomalies *etc.*," *op. cit.*, p. 70.

[17] From Nicholas J. Eastman: "Habitual Abortion,"
op. cit., p. 263.

[18] These statistics on premature birth, stillbirth, in-
fant mortality, are taken from the National Resources
Planning Board: "Human Conservation," March 1943
(U.S. Govt. Printing Office), pp. 29 and 39.

[19] A study in New York City revealed that 33 percent
of all crippled children interviewed had been disabled
at birth, due to congenital abnormalities or birth in-
juries. This suggests that prevention of such crippling
will come through improved methods of delivery and
through preventing pathologies of the ova which result
in such congenital abnormalities. See Report of the
Commission for Study of Crippled Children: *The Crippled Child in New York City*, 1940, pp. 15-16.

[20] R. M. Yerkes: *Chimpanzees*, p. 241.

[21] *Ibid.*, p. 243.

22 National Resources Planning Board, *op. cit.*, p. 30. While the death rate has been reduced by over two-thirds for children in the tenth month of life (3.1 per 100 live births in 1920 to 0.9 in 1939), the number of deaths in the first day of life has been reduced hardly at all in twenty years (14.7 per 100 live births in 1920 and 13.8 in 1939). *Ibid.*, p. 39. This suggests a neglect of potential safeguards during the prenatal period.

23 N. J. Eastman: "The Aims of Birth Control, *etc.*," *op. cit.*, p. 275.

24 R. M. Yerkes: *Chimpanzees*, p. 240.

25 Michael J. Bennett and P. B. Russell, Jr.: "Vaginal Smears Correlated to Ovarian Function," *The Southern Surgeon*, v. 10, 1941, pp. 79-87.

acknowledgments

Acknowledgment is made to the publishers, authors and copyright owners for permission to quote from the following books: HUMAN SEX ANATOMY, Robert L. Dickinson (Baillière, Tindall & Cox); CASTE AND CLASS IN A SOUTHERN TOWN, John Dollard (Yale University Press); THE COMING AMERICAN FASCISM, Lawrence Dennis (Harper and Brothers); BODILY CHANGES IN PAIN, HUNGER, FEAR AND RAGE, Walter B. Cannon (D. Appleton-Century Company); CHIMPANZEES, Robert M. Yerkes (Yale University Press); THE SEX TECHNIQUE IN MARRIAGE, I. E. Hutton (Emerson Books, Inc.); THE SEX FACTOR IN MARRIAGE, Helena Wright (Williams & Norgate Ltd.); THE PHYSIOLOGY OF SEX, Kenneth Walker (Penguin Books Ltd.); THE COLLECTED POETRY OF W. H. AUDEN (Faber & Faber Ltd.); W, e. e. cummings (Liveright Publishing Corp.); OUR SEX LIFE, Fritz Kahn (Wm. Heinemann Ltd.); WOMEN AND MEN, Amram Scheinfeld (Chatto & Windus); INTRODUCTORY LECTURES ON PSYCHOANALYSIS, Sigmund Freud (Allen & Unwin Ltd.); PROGRESS IN GYNECOLOGY, "Habitual Abortion," Nicholas J. Eastman (Grune and Stratton, Inc.); LOVE AGAINST HATE, Karl A. Menninger (Allen & Unwin Ltd.); PROCEEDINGS OF THE CONFERENCE ON PROBLEMS OF HUMAN FERTILITY, 1943, 'The Age of Corpora Lutea and Timing of Ovulation,' William W. Greulich, Edward S. Morris and Marion E. Black (National Committee on Maternal Health, George Banta Publishing Co., Menasha, Wisconsin); MANUAL OF HUMAN EMBRYOLOGY, edited by Franz Keibel and F. P.

Mall, "The Pathology of the Human Ovum," F. P. Mall
(J. B. Lippincott Company); MARRIAGE, Ernest R.
Groves (Henry Holt and Company); BEYOND GOOD AND
EVIL, Friedrich Nietzsche, Trans. Zimmern (Allen & Un-
win Ltd.); PHOENIX: POSTHUMOUS PAPERS OF D. H. LAW-
RENCE (Wm. Heinemann Ltd.); BEHAVIOUR AND NEU-
ROSIS, Jules H. Masserman (University of Chicago
Press); A THOUSAND MARRIAGES, Robert L. Dickinson
and Lura Beam (Baillière, Tindall & Cox).